THE CASE FOR
ASTRAL PROJECTION

By Sylvan Muldoon

**Author of "The Projection
of the Astral Body," etc.**

The Aries Press

GEORGE ENGELKE

CHICAGO · 1936

Second Printing

Printed in the U.S.A.

"It argues ill for the boasted freedom of opinion among scientific men, that they have so long refused to institute a scientific investigation into the existence and nature of facts asserted by so many competent and credible witnesses, and which they are freely invited to examine when they please. For my part 1 too much value the pursuit of truth, and the discovery of any new fact in nature, to avoid inquiry because it appears to clash with prevailing opinions."

SIR. WILLIAM CROOKES

"IN MANY INSTANCES, AT THE TIME OF DEATH OR OF GREAT DANGER . . . THE DYING MAN OR VICTIM OF AN ACCIDENT, EVEN WHEN SUCH ACCIDENT IS NOT FOLLOWED BY DEATH, APPEARS TO A FRIEND IN HIS USUAL ASPECT. THE PHANTOM GENERALLY REMAINS SILENT. SOMETIMES HE SPEAKS OR ANNOUNCES HIS DEATH."

DR. ALEXIS CARREL—*Man, the Unknown.*

PREFACE

I need say little concerning my purpose in presenting this volume, for the title itself aptly conveys my object, viz., to set forth evidence to establish the case for astral projection, which I consider, not a religious, but a strictly scientific problem.

Except for one instance, I have not resorted to quoting my own experiences in establishing this case—for two very good reasons: In the first place, many of my past experiences were recorded in my first *technical* book, *The Projection of the Astral Body*, and my more recent will soon appear in my second *technical* work, where they will be used as a basis of explanation. Secondly, in setting forth a case, the quoting of one's own personal experiences is often looked upon by the more critical as a fabrication, to strengthen one's contentions.

As the early researchers, backed by the Society for Psychical Research (referred to briefly by the initials, S. P. R.) made an extensive census of hallucinations, that is, recorded the testimony of persons claiming to have *seen* phantasms of the living, I have, during available time and on my own resources, been collecting testimony from persons claiming to have *been* phantoms—to have had out-of-the-body experiences.

In this first non-technical volume I have tried to gather together under one cover, for ready reference of future researchers, not only the more notable published cases along this line which have been scattered here and there; but also cases from my own private collection. Many of the latter have been secured at great expenditure of time and labor, by extensive correspondence, cross-correspondence and personal interviews. Yet they comprise only a portion of the total I have up to date recorded.

Since I am not sustained by any organization and intend to continue building up a large census of these experiences, ultimately to be published, I urge any of my readers who have or may come in contact with such cases to join with me in bringing them to light. In this connection, any communication will reach me at my home address: Darlington, Wisconsin.

In conclusion I take this opportunity to thank those individuals who have already forseen the great value of bringing forth a census of this kind and have contributed their experiences toward it, for it may eventually form a working basis on which our conservative scientists will venture to attain experimental proof of the spiritual nature of man and the problem of survival.

S. M.

TABLE OF CONTENTS

12

14

PART ONE

A SPIRITUAL BODY IN MAN

The belief that every human being possesses a spiritual body is age old and, in truth, the foundation of practically all religions. Man's spiritual body has been designated by any number of names—spirit, subtle body, entity, astral body, etheric body, the desire body, the luminous body, the fluidic body, the double, the finer body, the phantom, the pneuma (Greek), the rauch (Hebrew), the Ka (Egyptian), and most commonly as the *ghost*.

Among the various branches of the occult there has always been some conflict over exactly how many of these finer bodies mortal man possesses and exactly how each is to be designated; but I have always believed that it would be much better and more scientific policy to concentrate on the accumulation of evidence for one of these bodies, determine its condition at death and immediately following, learn if possible its true status and inter-relation with the physical, instead of arguing about the other half dozen and theorizing about the ultimate fate of the soul thousands of years from now.

So, for the purpose of this book, I shall use any or all of the above mentioned terms synonymously—spirit, astral body, phantom, ghost, etc., meaning one and the same.

As I have said, such a belief is age old. The Indian's spirit, at death, went to the happy hunting ground. The ancient Egyptians believed in a spiritual principle in man which they called the Ka, and it was this Ka, which, after the physical body was dead and mummified, visited it from time to time. Many of the older Egyptian paintings picture their conception of the Ka as a sort of bird-like double of the deceased.

In the lately translated Tibetan *Book of the Dead*, edited by Dr. W. Y. Evans-Wentz—the Bardo Thödol—believed to have

17

been written in the eighth century A. D. and embodying teachings thought by experts to be about two centuries older, the idea that man contains a spirit is emphasized at great length.

While many people, especially churchgoers, shun all investigation into the true nature of man, it has nevertheless always been quite generally believed by those same people that the spirit survives bodily death. And, while the word *ghost* is considered rather taboo and ridiculous when mentioned by a scientific researcher, thousands hold the word in high esteem when speaking of how Christ "gave up the ghost" on Calvary.

DISCOVERIES OF EARLY PSYCHICAL RESEARCHERS

Years ago, when the early members of the Society for Psychical Research—Myers, Gurney, Podmore, Barrett, the Sidgwicks, and others, first began their investigations into alleged spirit manifestations, telepathy, sleep, dreams, hypnotism, and numerous other allied subjects, they were literally amazed at the immensity of the testimony pertaining to ghosts of the dead, ghosts of the dying, and more startling still, *ghosts of the living*—ghosts of persons still living in the flesh!

Actually hundreds of sane and practical people were examined, questioned, and cross-examined, who steadfastly maintained that they had seen ghosts. Those critical, yet broadminded, researchers discovered, for example, that there were a great number of ghosts appeared to others at the time of death, even prior to death, and that ghosts of the living appeared and depicted some condition, for instance, tragical, of the person they represented. The statements of those claiming to have seen ghosts of the living were given rigorous scrutiny.

The result of the first Census, published in *Phantasms of the Living,* and the second and far more extensive one published in Vol. X. of the *S. P. R. Proceedings,* confirmed the belief that such perception of phantoms was more than chance could account for; that there was some connection between the apparition and the person whose ghost was seen, that these claims could not be laughed or ridiculed away. So, forty years ago, phantoms of the living was the all-absorbing issue among psychical researchers.

The person whose double appeared some distance from his actual physical habitat was designated as the *agent*. The seer of the ghost was referred to as the *percepient*.

Mr. Myers and Mr. Podmore carried their investigations much farther than their colleagues, and it is interesting to note that their opinions as to how phantoms of living persons were brought about and seen by others, were at variance. The fact alone that those two men, working together, disagreed in their postulations shows conclusively that they were searchers for the truth and not conspiring to deceive the public.

Each of those great thinkers incorporated his views in subsequent volumes. Myers brought forth *Human Personality and its Survival of Bodily Death*. Mr. Podmore's ideas were recorded in his, *Apparitions and Thought Transference*.

To show how these two really ingenious men differed in their explanations of the phenomenon, let us turn for a moment to their records and notice how each commented upon the same case. The case is one in which a physically alive mother (Mrs. Alexander) paid a ghostly visit to her sick daughter (Helen Alexander)—miles away— and was seen by the latter's nurse whose name was Frances Reddell. I abbreviate the statement of the percepient, Frances Reddell.

Antony, Torpoint
14th December, 1882

"Helen Alexander......was lying here very ill with typhoid fever, and was attended by me. I was standing at the table by her bedside, pouring out her medicine, at about four o'clock in the morning. . . . I heard the call-bell ring (this had been heard twice before during the night in the same week) and was attracted by the door of the room opening, and by seeing a

19

person entering the room whom I instantly felt to be the mother of the sick woman.

"She had a brass candlestick in her hand, a red shawl over her shoulders, and a flannel petticoat on which had a hole in the front. I looked at her as much as to say, 'I am glad you have come,' but the woman looked at me sternly, as much as to say, 'Why wasn't I sent for before?'

"I gave the medicine to Helen Alexander, and then turned round to speak to the vision—but no one was there! She had gone! She was a short dark person and very stout. At about six o'clock that morning Helen Alexander died. Two days later her parents and a sister came to Antony, and arrived between one and two o'clock in the morning; I and another maid let them in, and it gave me a great turn when I saw the living likeness of the vision I had seen two nights before!

"I told the sister (of Helen Alexander) about the vision, and she said that the description of the dress exactly answered to her mother's and that they had brass candlesticks at home exactly like the one I had described......"

Signed: Frances Reddell

Frances Reddell's story was corroborated by the mistress of the house where Helen Alexander died, Mrs. Pole-Carew, who testified that Frances Reddell had described the ghostly visitor to her shortly after seeing it. Further strength is given the incident by the fact that Miss Reddell had never had any odd experience of the sort before. The Hon. Mrs. Lyttelton, formerly of Selwyn College, Cambridge, testified that Miss Reddell was a most practical and matter of fact person and was particularly impressed by the fact that she saw a hole in the (ghost) mother's flannel petticoat, made by the busk of her stays. The description of the ghost and all other details tallied with the description of the actual living mother.

Mr. Podmore offered the following conjecture: "The simplest explanation and that which involves the least departure from known forms of telepathy is that the figure seen by Frances Reddell was due to thought transference from the mind of the dying girl."

Mr. Myers comments on the same case:

"Now what I imagine to have happened here is this. The mother, anxious about her daughter, paid her a psychical visit during the sleep of both. In so doing, she actually modified a certain position of space, not materially nor optically, but in such a manner that persons perceptive in a certain fashion would discern in that part of space the conception of her own aspect latent in the invading mother's mind."

It is obvious that Mr. Podmore had a sentiment for trying to rule out spiritism and try to account for such phenomena by mind and telepathy alone. (Professor Charles Richet later tried to explain these phenomena with a similar sentiment, a theory he called the *sixth sense*.) On the other hand Myers' writings all hint at the fact that he believed something more than a thought traveled from agent to percepient—that it was a projection of some portion of the agent's spiritual element.

Personally I am convinced that these men were correct to a certain degree, and wrong—all of them wrong—to a certain degree, that they were making the mistake of trying to make their "pet theories" fit every case where phantoms of the living were seen.

I realize it will ire many of my Spiritualist and Theosophist friends to hear me say anything good for Richet or Podmore, after all I have written concerning the astral body and its reality, but the truth is this: There are cases, multitudes of them, where an idea like Mr. Podmore's or Mr. Richet's seems most fitting; and there are other cases where the projection of the astral body appears most logical; and still others where *no* single explanation covers the facts.

There are *arrival cases*, where the phantom of the living person is seen arriving at a certain place long before he actually arrives physically. There are cases where the apparition of the living person is seen *collectively*—by several persons at the same time; where the apparition is seen *repeatedly* by *different persons,* or may be seen several times by the same persons. And cases where the living person sees his own phantasm. Space permitting, we will cite examples of these cases later; I wish to repeat, however, that regardless of all the postulations set forth up to date, not one of them is valid enough to explain all cases.

Since my own experiments and researches over a period of years have been especially directed to the phenomenon known as the projection of the astral body, and since that phenomenon does account for *many* of these cases of ghosts of the living, we will for the present ignore any other supposition—such as Richet's *sixth sense* or Podmore's *telepathic hallucinations*— regardless of their worth and turn directly to our subject. First I feel that a brief description of astral projection will be in order, mostly for the benefit of those readers unfamiliar with the matter.

DOCTRINE OF ASTRAL PROJECTION*

Generally speaking, the doctrine of astral projection is that every human being is made up of two counterparts—the material and the non-material or ghost. The ghost is the vehicle of consciousness, containing the energy of life and more truly the real man than the physical body.

This ghost counterpart is capable, under certain conditions. such as syncope, trance, while fainting, while under the influence of an anaesthetic, during sleep, etc., of entirely withdrawing from its physical abode and traveling about as a complete and separate entity.

Many claim to have seen the ghost hovering about the death-bed. Such ghosts are intangible to physical objects and, while

*Much of this explanation is from my own original discoveries.—S. M.

usually invisible, they have sometimes been seen many miles away from their physical bodies.

The composition of the ghost self is, I feel, not definitely known at present. By some investigators it is thought to be *fluidic*. Sir Oliver Lodge believes it to be *etheric*.* Others are of the opinion that it is composed of highly refined matter— atoms and electrons vibrating at infinitely high velocities.

At all times during projection, the ghost is in communication with its physical counterpart by means of a line-of-force—a sort of elastic cord, across which flows the vital energy sustaining life in the unconscious body.

Like the astral body, the line-of-force is designated by a large number of names, such as, the astral cord, the astral cable, the silver cord, the psychic cord, the vital intermediary, the fluidic cord, and others. In color it is grey and although capable of infinite expansion, it may not be severed during the projection of the ghost without causing certain and instantaneous death to the physical body.

There are two types of projections—*involuntary* and *voluntary*. In the former, the subject, through no effort of his own, suddenly awakens to find himself conscious in a phantom body, a ghost for the time being— a ghost of a living person! In the voluntary type the subject actually projects himself outside of his physical body and becomes a ghost at will.

I would not have you believe, however, that ghosts of the living are always conscious, for the projected phantom can also be *partially* conscious (dreaming) or fully unconscious. When the ghost is traveling about outside the body in an unconscious state the condition is known as astral somnambulism and is similar to physical somnambulism or sleep-walking.

The ghost, in a state of astral somnambulism can perform activities of the most unbelievable type—not only re-enact

---

*In this connection see, *The Human Atmosphere,* by Dr. Walter J. Kilner, especially pp 2 and 43.

23

events which have occurred to the subject in the past but also enact some which are destined to occur in the future! For years, students of the occult have been fascinated by the prophetic dream; yet here is a phenomenon far more amazing, for the projected ghost enacts the future event, often in its true locale.

The route the phantom travels while exteriorizing from the physical body is as a rule specific. When one is in a lying-down position, or horizontally at rest, the astral body advances from the physical in an upward and outward direction while remaining parallel to the latter.

After attaining a height of anywhere from three to six feet above its shell, the phantom, still horizontal, will either upright itself there or begin to move itself along on the air for perhaps several yards, then upright, or come down into a standing position some distance from its earthly counterpart. Sometimes the phantom projects in a "spiral spin" and occasionally the sensation is reversed, i. e., when ascending the subject feels he is descending.

Being thus projected entirely out of the physical and upright the phantom is now able to travel about in the immediate vicinity or far away. In my former work I fully discussed the several methods by which the phantom moves and will not go into that again, except to say that in traveling to distant places time and space have no bearing upon the matter as the ghost is functioning on the fourth dimension.

*It must be kept in mind that these projections are controlled by a seeming superior intelligence which appears to be innate in or directed to the subject.** By way of explanation, let us suppose that, in the case of Mrs. Alexander, visiting her dying daughter, and being seen by the nurse, Frances Reddell, the ghost seen was the projected astral body of Mrs. Alexander.

---

*The astral body is not held to be the soul, but one of the vehicles of the soul.

Remember, this is only a supposition, for no one knows whether the case was one of projection or not.

If such were the case, it was the super-normal faculties of Mrs. Alexander's mind which knew of the daughter's illness, caused the exteriorization, caused the phantom to travel. This super-normal or super-conscious mind so far transcends explanation as to be omnipotent.

When one is asleep, the senses are often particularly keen and it is the specific maneuvering of the slumbering astral self (that is, upward and outward on the air) which brings on many of those peculiar dreams of rising, falling, floating, flying, etc., which have so long puzzled psychologists.

Often when the astral body is in the air above the physical, the subject will begin to grow conscious as it descends into the latter and experience a "falling-dream"—one of those dreams which our *dream experts* try to explain away as the result of weak bed-springs or as symbolizing a falling off of business, etc.

LITERATURE ON THE SUBJECT

Up to the time of the appearance of the book, *The Projection of the Astral Body*, in 1929, practically nothing of any value concerning actual *projection* had ever been published, although the literature of occultism fairly abounds in works about the astral plane, the astral body and the like. In summing up this literature I can do nothing better than reproduce the words of Dr. Carrington verbatim, from his *Introduction* to the before-mentioned book:

"Much has been written, in the past, concerning the Astral Body—mostly in books devoted to Magic and Occultism. I believe I have gone through the majority of such books carefully, in my endeavor to find some practical information bearing upon this question (of projection) but with little result. Thus there are numerous references to the astral body in e. g. Eliphas Levi's *Doctrine and Ritual of Magic*, in his

Key of the Mysteries (published in The Equinox, Vol. X.) ; in A. E. Waite's, *Mysteries of Magic,* and his *Occult Sciences;* in Dr. Franz Hartman's, *Magic, White and Black,* and in the various writings of Paracelsus.

"In the older works upon Sorcery and Witchcraft there are, of course, frequent allusions to astral projection. Theosophical literature is full of this subject, but even here I have been unable to find anywhere precise information (of actual projection) ......This is true not only of the older books, such as Leadbeater's, *The Astral Plane,* and Annie Besant's, *Man and his Bodies,* but also the newer and more voluminous treatises, such as those of Major Arthur E. Powell—*The Etheric Body, The Astral Body, The Mental Body,* etc.

"In all these books, much theoretical information is given (of course, from the strictly Theosophical point of view) but very little practical advice. The same criticism applies to D'Assier's book *Posthumous Humanity: A Study of Phantoms.* Some interesting spontaneous experiences are given in *Little Journeys into the Invisible: A Woman's Actual Experiences in the Fourth Dimension,* by M. Gifford Shine; *Some Occult Experiences,* by Johan van Manen; *My Travels in the Spirit World,* by Caroline D. Larsen, and in other books of the kind; while some curious lore of a general nature is contained in *The Astral Light* by Nizida.

"An interesting historical study of this subject is given in G. R. S. Mead's, *Doctrine of the Subtle Body in Western Tradition,* in which he summarizes the views of the early Fathers, as well as later conceptions. Charles Hallock's book *Luminous Bodies: Here and Hereafter,* contains little to the point. Occasional references to what Mr. Myer's (in his *Human Personality;* called 'Self Projection' may be found scattered through the *Journals* and *Proceedings* of the S. P. R. . . . Mr. A. Campbell Holmes has some remarks upon the Double in his *Facts of Psychic Science and Philosophy,* while I have devoted chapters to the subject in my *Modern Psychical Phenomenon* and *Higher Psychical Development*. Several years ago, Mr. Prescot Hall published in the *Journal* of the A. S. P. R. a number of communications of considerable interest, which he had received regarding the astral body through the instrumentality of a blind medium. Their value, of course, depends altogether upon the authenticity of their source.

"This is practically all of the published material which I have been enabled to find . . . with the exception of Mr. Oliver Fox's articles in the *Occult Review*, and two books in French. These are: *Le Fantome des Vivants*, by H. Durville, and *Methode de Deboublement Personnel* (Exterioration de la Neuricite: Sorties en Astral) by M. Charles Lancelin.

. . . As I have said, with these exceptions, I have found practically nothing of value in the entire literature of the subject . . ."

To the foregoing list I would add two small books, *The Astral World* by Swami Panchadasi; *The Guiding Power* by George Starr White, M. D., and a small booklet *Astral Travels* by "Helen," all of a utopian nature; also *Practical Astral Projection* translated from the French by Yram. Besides *The Projection of the Astral Body* and several magazine articles by myself, two articles recently appeared in Prediction Magazine, one by Wm. Gerhardi (March 1936) and another by Dr. Nandor Fodor (June 1936).

BILOCATION ANALOGOUS TO PROJECTION

To go back into history we find that the Christian Church described a phenomenon analogous to the projection of the astral body which was termed *bilocation*.

From St. Paul's testimony we have reason to assume that he sometimes experienced bilocation, or the faculty of being physically present in one place and spiritually present in another. It will be recalled too that St. Paul in his first *Epistle to the Corinthians* said: "There is a natural (physical) body and there is a spiritual body."

While preaching in the Church of St. Pierre du Queyroix at

Limoges on Holy Thursday in the year 1226, St. Anthony of Padua remembered that he was due at the very time at services in a monastery some distance away. So, while the congregation, to which he was preaching, waited, he knelt down, drew his hood over his head, and apparently transferred himself to the monastery astrally;—for at the very time, St. Anthony was seen by the assembled monks to step forth into their monastery chapel, read his appointed passage and vanish!

According to the researcher Dr. Nandor Fodor, LLD., similar stories are recorded of Severus of Ravanna, St. Ambrose, and St. Clement of Rome. Fodor further says: "Perhaps the best known case of this type (bilocation or projection) is dated September 17th, 1774. Alphonse de Liguori, imprisoned at Arezzo, remained quiet in his cell and took no nourishment. Five days later he awoke in the morning and said that he had been at the death-bed of Pope Clement XLV. His statement was confirmed. He was seen in attendance by the bedside of the dying Pope!"

A PARALLEL IN MESMERISM

Ordinarily we comprehend *consciousness* as being a function of the physical brain. The Materialistic conception is that the brain oozes thought, just as the liver oozes bile. While, as I pointed out in the beginning, millions believe they survive the decay of the physical brain, for the most part we cannot conceive of consciousness, of one being consciously aware of his feelings, thinking sanely, able to describe his sensations, apart from his physical brain. Yet, when Andrew Jackson Davis allowed himself to be mesmerized, his description shows that his conscious mind was functioning without the use of his physical brain or nerve tracts.

Notice especially that Davis says he *could not* use his physical organs; that he *could not* even move his tongue. But at the same time, some mentality (other than his consciousness) was giving messages through his physical organism.

At the time Davis was a young lad working in a store in the village of Poughkeepsie. I now let Davis tell his own story, from *The Magic Staff*:

" . . . . William Levingston called at the store. During a recital of many magnetic marvels he had himself performed, both at home and abroad, he addressed himself to me and said: 'Have you ever been mesmerized?' In reply I informed him of an unsuccessful experiment upon me by Mr. Grimes. Then he said: 'Come to my house tonight. I'll try you, if you don't object, and Edwin too.' There was no reason for declining and I therefore accepted his invitation.

"Before relating what happened on that memorable night, however, I wish to call attention to the fact, that having no confidence in the alleged phenomena of mesmerism, I was actuated simply by what seemed to me to be the suggestion of the moment—just like others whose curiosity had become superficially excited.

" . . . . I felt the operator's chilly hands pass and re-pass my brow . . . Anon, all was intensely dark within. Dreadful and strange feelings passed over my body and through my brain. My emotions were painful . . . I had horrid convictions of what the world calls Death. 'Oh mother!' thought I with terror, can this be the period of my physical dissolution?

"My heart continued to perform its office; but its beatings were less frequent. I felt the different senses that connect the mind with the outer world gradually closing. 'Alas!' methought desparingly, are they closing forever? . . . . . . I could no longer hear the busy and active world without, nor feel the touch of any object, living or dead. No longer, thought I, can I behold the system of nature. The fragrant fields are gone, never more to be the scenes of happy contemplation.

" . . . . Thoughts like these flashed through my awestruck mind. What am I to do?"

Davis goes on at great length to describe the sensations and emotions he was experiencing, much of which I here omit.

Eventually he resolved, within himself, to try to regain his normal physical status. He said, to himself:

" 'I will submit no longer to this dangerous and dreadful experiment. Never again shall my marvel-seeking self lead me into such pitfalls. Yes, I will speak and protest against this dreadful operation!....But oh, how frightful! My tongue seemed instantly to be enlarged and clung to the roof of my mouth. My cheeks seemed extremely swollen and my lips were joined as if by death, apparently to move no more.

"Another resolution passed through my brain and instantly I obeyed its suggestion. I made a desperate effort to change my position—particularly to disengage my hands—but (horrible beyond description!) *my feet, my hands, my whole body, were entirely beyond the control of my volition.** I could no longer claim proprietorship over my own person. All was lost, it seemed, irretrievably lost. I felt convinced that external life was for me no more. What could I do?

"*True, I could exercise my mental faculties to the highest degree—could reason with a startling alertness—but could not hear, see, feel, speak, or move......*I queried and reasoned within myself thus: I have a body— a tangible body—I resided in the *form—but is it my natural or spiritual body? Is* it adapted to the outer world, or to post-mortem life? Where am I? I am so lonely. Alas, if this be death!........What surprised me more than anything else was the gushing forth of novel and brilliant thoughts—extending apparently over the vast landscape of some unknown world of indescribable beauty.

" . . . . Presently all was dark as before . . . Death seemed inevitable. Every moment I approached nearer and nearer to a mysterious dark valley . . . Again and again I retreated in my mind, but every thought wafted me nearer that fearful vale of inconceivable darkness. I was filled with terror.

" . . . . Suddenly, with an unearthly shudder and terrible to

---

*See Astral Catalepsy in The Projection of the Astral Body, pp 10-11

30

relate—I found myself whirling . . . I seemed to be revolving in a spiral path, with a wide sweep at first, and then smaller; so that every revolution, on my descending flight, contracted the circle of my movement . . . I awoke to physical consciousness, mentally revolving in a circuitous form . . . sound vibrated through the labyrinths of my ears, sensation flashed over my whole frame.

" . . . . But how joyfully surprised. I was precisely in the same condition as when I had seated myself for the experiment! . . . I could remember nothing except my mental suffering; and, somehow, in my bewilderment, I did not feel quite certain that I had not died. I could not realize that I had, in reality, returned from the dark valley of death. But a few penetrating glances about the room and upon the familiar faces of those around, convinced me. . . . .whereupon I arose and greeted the amazed and delighted witnesses."

"What is the matter?" Davis asked. "What brought these folks here?" "I sent for them," replied the operator, "to see you perform". "Perform!" Davis gasped.

'Yes—perform. You're a queer youth to be sure.' Levingston said, 'but I know what your Power is called . . . .It is called Clairvoyance by Chancey Hare Townsend. I have read his book on *Facts in Mesmerism* in which he describes cases of seeing blindfolded, just as you have done here tonight to perfection.' "

Davis was puzzled at the operator's statements. "What's been done," he inquired. "Tell me about it."

Levingston replied: "Why you read from your forehead the large letters on the newspaper; told time by our watches. . . . . besides you described where some of us are diseased, all to our perfect satisfaction."

Davis tells how he repeated the mesmeric sittings with Mr. Levingston and became the object of both reverence and scorn among his townsfolk. He no longer experienced throes at the dreadful intermediate state but passed, in less than thirty min-

31

utes, into a very pleasant state of mental existence. In the chapter *My First Flight Through Space* he wrote: "As usual my mind was rendered incapable of controlling the slightest muscle, or of realizing any definite sensation except a kind of waving fluctuation. . . .This was a very strange sensation, but not unpleasant, but in a few moments I passed into the most delightful state of tranquility . . . I was completely born again in the spirit. My thoughts were most peaceful. My whole nature was completely expanded."

It may be only coincidence, but is it not a remarkable coincidence, that Mr. Davis tells of being disengaged from his physical body while magnetized, while Mr. Cleave tells of being seen in a phantom body while magnetized? Is it coincidence or is the magnetic trance apropos to astral projection?

Mr. Cleave and his friend Mr. Sparks were naval engineering students at Plymouth and were known by the researchers Myers and Gurney. They relate the following story:

"Sparks, magnetized his friend Cleave who had expressed a desire to see a young lady living at Woodsworth and to be seen by her. Cleave, after about twenty minutes' magnetic sleep, declared that he had seen the lady, that she had looked at him and had placed her hands over her eyes. Three days afterwards, on the 18th of January, the experiment was repeated. The magnetized Cleave declared that he imagined he had frightened the lady . . . On the following day, Cleave received a letter from the young lady . . . She declared that on Friday she had been terrified at the sight of Cleave walking into her room. She had thought that it might be a vision of her imagination. On the following Monday, however, she had been even more alarmed at seeing him again, very distinctly."

SIMILARITY OF PROJECTION TO HINDU SAMADHI

In the past it is possible that hundreds of persons have been buried alive, that is, prior to the modern methods of embalming now generally practiced. Cases of suspended animation, projection, deep-trance could easily have been mistaken for death by the hasty, when, as a matter of fact, the ghost may have returned.

Anne Carter Lee, the mother of General Robert E. Lee, was pronounced dead in October 1805 and laid to rest in the family mausoleum. Seven days later an elderly sexton, bringing flowers into the burial-place, heard a voice from the tomb. Terrified, he informed the family. They entered the mausoleum and discovered that the woman was alive! She recovered completely from this horrifying experience which occurred two years before the birth of Robert E. Lee! One collector has reported five hundred and eighty cases of this sort (suspended animation).

There are in India certain Hindus who can bring on this state of apparent death voluntarily. Samadhi they call it and it seems to be a self-induced catalepsy—an intermediate state between life and death, so akin to the latter in fact that the subject can actually be buried.

A most extraordinary case of this kind occurred many years ago when a yogi from the Province of Lahore named Haridas was buried for a period of thirty days. Haridas, after entering the state of samadhi, was placed in a securily tied sack, the sack then placed in a box which was locked, the keys being deposited with the British General. The box was then placed in a brick vault, the door of which was sealed with Prince Ranjeet Singh's seal and a guard of British soldiers stood watch over the vault day and night.

Thirty days later the vault was opened, box unlocked, sack untied, and the yogi, very emancipated was resusticated by his friends. This test was conducted under the strict supervision of Sir. Claude Wade and Raja Ranjeet Singh.

Hamid Bey who has startled the Western world with his demonstrations has undertaken several prolonged public burials while in a state of samadhi. He remained buried an hour in Atlanta, Ga.; three hours in Englewood, N. J.; seven hours

33

in San Diego, Cal, etc.—without any coffin, having been placed directly in the ground, with the earth covering his face and body—in the presence of sceptical newspaper men. Accounts of these burials were published in the press at the time and are available to anyone interested.

A more recent statement vouching for voluntary suspended animation comes from Upton Sinclair the brilliant playwright, novelist, politician and publicist, published in July 1936,* in which he tells of a friend of his who came daily to his house and gave amazing demonstrations. While Sinclair offers no explanation he says in all sincerity:

"He had the ability to produce anaesthesia in many parts of his body and stick hat-pins through his tongue and cheeks without pain; he could go into a deep trance in which his body became rigid and cold. Once I put his head on one chair and his heels on another and stood in the middle as if he were a two inch plank. We have a motion picture film showing a 150 lb. rock being broken with a sledge-hammer on his abdomen while he lay in this trance.

"The vital functions were so far suspended in this trance that he could be shut up in an air-tight coffin and buried underground for several hours; nor was there any 'hocus-pocus' about this—I know physicians who got the coffins and arranged for the tests and watched every detail. In Ventura, California, it was done in a ball park and a game of ball played over the grave. . . . ."

Numerous travellers and investigators, returning from the Orient—India, Egypt, and other Eastern countries, have reported similar cases. The occultists, of course, maintain that during these burials, the body of sensation—the astral body— is projected from its material form, and the latter, though still attached to the astral cord—survives by its vegetative functioning; that enough vital energy reaches the body by way of cord to prevent complete expiration.

---

*Prediction Magazine

On the other hand, the average critic will probably say that these spectacular performances never take place at all, that the witnesses were deluded by magic or magicians. In nine cases out of ten such critics know nothing about samadhi or magic either. Thus their opinions are of little value. So, let us take the testimony of a man who is qualified, by experience, to speak—the world famous magician, Howard Thurston.

Thurston made an extensive and sceptical investigation of the matter and stated emphatically that samadhi is not trickery. He personally collected and enumerated weighty evidence along this line which he published a few years ago and startled the world by telling how ghosts of the living and ghosts of persons apparently dead were seen far from their physical forms which they later re-entered, and he expressed a suggestion that projection of the astral body was the explanation.

Thurston, who was acclaimed a master of the occult mysteries of India, tells how he made the acquaintance of several native gentlemen who were firm believers in the occult powers of yogi and claimed to have witnessed many unusual exhibitions.

He says:*

"In the annals of Ghosts, the theory exists that an etherial form is freed from the body after death and can make itself evident and visible. The Hindus believe that this action also transpires during the samadhi, but that the freed form is later able to resume its place in the body. This is something that psychic investigators have had little opportunity to study. . . . The question is intriguing. People say they have seen ghosts of those who have passed on. Have any of them seen ghosts of those who have *not* passed on, but are suspended in this strange state that is neither life nor death? *Yes,* and I shall give instances of actual cases. All have been at least partially corroborated by more than one person, and I am convinced that my informants were sincere. . . . . ."

*True Ghost Stories

Mr. Thurston tells of a yogi who, during samadhi, was buried at Delhi for a period of eight days. During that time his double was seen in Bombay! The truth of the incident is strengthened by the testimony of several witnesses whom Mr. Thurston questioned.

Again he tells how a yogi occasionally came to the house of a wealthy Calcutta native to receive gifts. The yogi later went North to the country from which he came.

"Two weeks later," Thurston's account goes on to state, "the yogi entered the room where the Calcutta man was sitting, gazed at him intently for a full minute, and then left, with neither greeting nor farewell. The Calcutta man was amazed, but convinced of the yogi's occult powers, felt sure he had seen a ghostly manifestation. He inquired in Calcutta and made sure the yogi had actually left town. Then he wrote to a friend in Northern India to inquire about the holy man. A few weeks later he received a reply which stated that the yogi *was* in Northern India and that he had just completed a term of samadhi. The Calcutta man was convinced he had seen the ghost of the man who was still alive! . . . I know of authentically reported cases in America which are more astounding than those I have just related. . . ."

He relates the case of Roger Martin, who, while in a state of apparent death in Chicago was seen—and talked to—by his sister Cynthia, in Philadelphia. The nurse, caring for Roger, stated that he had lapsed into a state of coma, after a sudden illness, two nights before, and that for several hours they had believed him dead. The period, described by the nurse, corresponded with the time of Cynthia's vision.

Thurston also tells of one, Benjamin Gough, of Ohio, who, from the age of sixteen was subject to deep trance spells and was often pronounced dead, by physicians called in. Several times Gough's projected ghost was seen elsewhere at the time of suspended animation. After relating several other cases, Thurston says: "This . . . trance condition seems very closely

36

related to the samadhi of India, although the Hindus assume it voluntarily. . . . .Yet of all the ghosts of which I have heard or read, these ghosts of the living seem to be the most remarkable."

SOME SCIENTIFIC EXPERIMENTS

Some years ago, Dr. Duncan McDougall, of Haverhill Mass., conducted some unique experiments in which he weighed a number of patients dying from consumption, at the moment of death. He placed the cot containing the patient on a delicately balanced scale—so that the patient (bed and all) was weighed. At the moment of death the beam of the balance went up and struck the upper arm suddenly. The weight thus lost was calculated and was found, in four out of six cases, to be between 2 and 2½ ounces.

Although the experiments of Prof. L. V. Twining in detecting a loss of weight in small animals at death were given considerable publicity, Mr. Twining writes this author that he does not consider his discoveries of much importance even though they were made under proper conditions at the Los Angeles Polytechnic Institute. So we will omit his testimony. Whether a loss of weight at the very moment of death is indicative of some substance leaving the body, I leave the reader to conclude for himself.*

In France, several prominent men of science, including Colonel Albert de Rochas, M. Charles Lancelin, M. Hector Durville, and others, claim to have extracted the astral body by hypnosis and mesmerism and to have performed many ingenious experiments with it.

Colonel Rochas claimed that with his subject in deep trance, he could, by suggestion, cause the etheric body to exteriorize in a sort of plastic form and unite into a phantasmal shape out-

---

*Dr. R. A. Watters, of the William Bernard Johnston Foundation, Reno, Nevada, claims to have successfully photographed "souls" of insects—mice etc., at the moment of death.

side the physical. The phantom, thus extracted, could be lengthened by the will of the operator, could pass through material things, was the seat of sensation, etc. When the Colonel suggested that the phantom take on her own mother's form the suggestion was carried out.

Durville, President of the Magnetic Society of France, in his book *Le Fantôme des Vivants*, deals with the subject at great length. His book is divided into two parts; part *one* being historical and explaining the general theory of the double. Part *two* sets forth his original experiments in which the astral body was apparently projected by mesmerism. For instance, Durville tells that the subject of the experiment is constantly *en rapport* with the double through the medium of the fluidic cord which is capable of elongation, the phantom is attired in a sort of gauze-like substance, sense impressions are conveyed across the cord, light is detrimental to success, etc.

In one chapter Durville states how calcium sulphide screens were placed some distance from the subject and the suggestion given that the phantom approach one of them. As a result that screen glowed up from the vital radiations emitted by the ghost when nearing it. Some other successes were reported by Durville such as moving the straw of a sthenometer by the exteriorized phantom. Some of this material is of absorbing interest and, according to Dr. Carrington, agrees remarkably with the descriptions and experiments set forth by the present writer elsewhere. Durville concludes his book as follows:

"Projection of the astral body is a certain fact, capable of being demonstrated by means of direct experiment. This also demonstrates to us that living force is independent of matter, and that our individuality is composed of a physical body and an intelligent soul and a vital link—the astral body. Since this phantom can exist and function apart from the physical body, it may also exist after death. That is, immortality is a fact which is proved scientifically."

The work of M. Charles Lancelin states that projection is

the result of externalization of neuric (nervous) energy and that the phantom is composed of this force. This outflowing of neuricity takes place in everyone, but very pronouncedly in some individuals, and is capable of being measured by delicately constructed instruments. Space forbids going into Lancelin's discoveries, suffice it to say, they corroborate the findings of other researchers in the same line.

Photographic evidence, that is photographing of the exteriorized phantom, is contained in the works of Rochas, Durville, Darget, Aksakof, Delanne, Ochorowicz and others. While this might, at first thought, seem preposterous, it is not unreasonable to suppose that the vital radiations of the energetic body can impress film, since the neural energy is akin to electricity and Professor Le Bon and colleagues have already shown that —by purely physical means—it is possible to stabilize and photograph electric current. Prof. Fukurai of the University of Tokio even brings forth strong evidence that *thought*—a form of energy—can be photographed, as does Dr. Baraduc.

At the Hague, two Dutch scientists (physicists)—Drs. Malta and Zaalberg Van Zelst tried to ascertain the chemical and molecular structure—the composition—of the astral body. Their conclusions, arrived at after prolonged experiment with such instruments as the dynamistograph, etc., were:

"The body is capable of contraction and expansion, under the action of the will—that is, the will of the astral body—the expansion being about 1.26mm., or about 1/40,000,000 of its own volume; its contraction being much greater—namely, about 8mm., or 1/6,250,000 of its volume. Its specific weight is about 12.24 mgs. lighter than hydrogen, and 176.5 times lighter than air.

"The will acts upon this body mechanically, causing it to expand (rise) and contract (descend) as the action takes place. It is thus subject to the law of gravity. There is an x force (unknown force) which holds the molecules of this body together. The atoms composing this body are extremely small widely separated and heavy. The internal density of the body is about the same as that of the external air. If the pressure of the air outside the body is increased, that inside the body will increase in exact proportion . . . The weight of this body was also calculated, and found by them to be about 69.5 gr.—approximately 2¼ oz." It should be noted that in the experiments of Dr. Duncan McDougall, the weight was estimated at about the same figure!

Many other prominent persons have been working either directly or indirectly on the problem of the vital principle in man. M. Yourievitch of the General Psychological Institute of Paris, and Dr. Sidney Alrutz, of Upsale University, Sweden, conducted experiments on the vital radiations from the human body, using all sorts of instruments. M. Yourievitch proved beyond a doubt the existence of what he termed "Y-rays." These rays emanate from all men and women.

Alrutz demonstrated with his apparatus that a curious force issued from the human hands which could pass through certain substances. Other tests have been made where photographic plates—wrapped in black paper to exclude light— and held against the subject's forehead, have, when developed, shown an image concentrated upon.

PERCEPIENTS WHO WITNESSED EXTERIORIZATION

In the literature of spiritism there have been from time to time stories from persons claiming to have seen the astral body (of persons other than themselves) exteriorized, or in the process of exteriorization, especially at the time of death. It is obvious that the truth of such testimony rests entirely with the person claiming to have seen the vision and cannot be corroborated. Andrew Jackson Davis in his *Harmonial Philosophy* gives the following description of one case which he observed:

"A human being lies. . . .dying. . . . .. .The physical body grows negative and cold, in proportion as the elements of the spiritual body become warm and positive. The feet become cold first. The clairvoyant sees right over the head what may be called a magnetic halo. . . . .golden in appearance and throbbing as though conscious.

"Now the body is cold up to the knees and elbows. The legs are then cold up to the hips and the arms to the shoulders. The emanation is more expanded, though it has not risen higher in the room. The death-coldness steals over the breast and around on either side. The emanation has attained a position near the ceiling. The person has ceased to breathe, the pulse is still.

"The emanation is elongated and fashioned in the outline of the human form. It is connected with the brain. The head of the person throbs internally—a slow deep throb, not painful but like the beat of the sea. The thinking faculties are rational, while nearly every part of the person is dead. The golden emanation is connected with the brain by a very fine life-thread.

"On the body of the emanation there appears something white and shining, like the human head; next comes a faint outline of the face divine; the fair neck and beautiful shoulders manifest, and then in rapid succession all parts of the new body down to the feet—a bright shining image, somewhat smaller than the physical, but a perfect prototype in all its details. . . . .The fine life-thread continues attached to the old brain. The next thing is the withdrawal of this electric principle. When the thread snaps the spiritual body is free. . . . ."

In the June 1936 issue of *Prediction Magazine* an article, which appears to have been written with sincere honesty by Dr. Riblet Brisbane Hout, tells how, on three different occasions, he saw the projected astral bodies of patients undergoing operations. This occurred, he says, while he was attending surgical clinic in a large hospital in Chicago, he being one of the three observers watching the operations. I abbreviate the Doctor's account:

"The entire personnel in the surgery that day were unaware

41

of the phenomena I saw before me. To them the patient was merely unconscious from deep inhalation of ether . . . I saw the spirit of the patient float free in space above the operating table, resting supine and inert . . . As the anaesthetic deepened . . . the freedom of the spirit became greater, for the form floated freely away from the physical counterpart . . . The spirit was quiet, as if in deep peaceful sleep.

"I know that the surgical activity was not affecting it, for the anaesthetic had driven it from the physical vehicle and it would remain separated from its body until the ether was lessened sufficient to allow its return. At the finish of this operation, while the wound was being closed the spirit came closer to the body but had not entered it when the patient was wheeled from the operating room . . . "

I will not here take the space to relate the other two visions of the exteriorized astral phantom which Dr. Hout states he saw except to say that one of them floated about horizontally in the room, while the other was upright and quite active. He continues: "Besides the spirit (astral body) I also saw spirit forms of others who were present watching the operating technique . . . I was able to see in each case, at least part of the time, the astral cord that united these spirit bodies with their physical counterparts. This was represented to me as a silvery shaft of light that wound around through the room in much the same way as a curl of smoke will drift indifferently in still atmosphere . . . "

In this connection I might mention at this juncture that only a few weeks ago an orthodox Methodist minister of irreproachable character, who has been well known in my neighborhood for years, confided in me that while at the bedside of a dying friend, early this spring, he saw a cloudlike light rise up out of the body of his friend just as the latter expired. The light, he stated, floated up into the air and disappeared.

Ignoring any criticism of T. K. (J. E. Richardson) it is interesting to read in his *Great Work*: "Three times within the last twenty years the writer has witnessed the phenomenon of the

separation of the spiritual body from the physical in the process
of death. In one of these instances the transit was that of his own
and only son . . . "

ALLEGED SPIRIT COMMUNICATIONS RELATING
TO ASTRAL BODY

A few statements, selected from many, alleged to have come
from spirits of the dead, by way of mediumship of diverse kinds,
give some interesting information relating to the astral body in
mortal man. We are told, for instance, that the spiritual or vital
energy never *wholly* leaves the material body during physical
life, even during projection—that there is always some portion
left therein. Commenting upon this in *Light*, Rev. Maitland says:

"This certainly bears out the communication purporting to
come from the spirit of F. W. H. Myers, through the hand of
Miss Cummins, in which he says that the whole of the astral body
never does leave the physical body during earth-life. The
essence, as he calls it, may dissociate itself for a time from the
physical body, but the bulk, or denser parts of the astral body
always remain behind, until death, joined to the finer parts
by the cord."

Dr. Hodgson, in his *Second Report on the Trance Phenomenon
of Mrs. Piper* (Proceedings, XIII, p. 400) says: "The statements of the 'communicators' as to what occurs on the physical
side may be put in brief general terms as follows: 'We all have
bodies composed of luminiferous ether enclosed in our flesh
and blood bodies. The relation of Mrs. Piper's etherical body
to the etherical world, in which the communicators claim to
dwell, is such that a special store of peculiar energy is accum-
ulated in connection with her organism, and this appears to them
as a *light* . . ."

Needless to tell any of you who are acquainted with the teachings of Spiritualism, Psychical Research, and Theosophy, that
spirits of the dead frequently speak of seeing mortals, especially

'psychics' as *lights*. This light which they see is in reality the radiations from the spiritual or luminous body.

J. M. Peebles, M. D., M. A., in his work *The Pathway of the Human Spirit* tells how he once asked a very exalted intelligence (spirit) some questions on this topic.

"Can you," asked Mr. Peebles, "while entrancing this medium, see the real spirit?"

'No, I can not. I can only sense and see the spiritual body.'

"When entrancing a mortal in the body, do you cause the owner to vacate it?"

'Not necessarily—entrancement is little more than mesmeric influence.'

"Can you really see—can you describe the unfleshed, unclothed spirit of this body?"

'I cannot. The most I can say through this instrument, is that it seems to be a very distinctly entity, *looking like a fiery diamond, a brilliant point of dazzling brightness shining through a very etherical white fluid,* connected in some way, sympathetically and vibratorially with the body that it owns.' "

In his book *Science and Personality,* William Brown, M. A., M. D., D. S. c., of the University of Oxford gives a report concerning the etheric body in man which he obtained at a seance with Mrs. Osborne Leonard, the famous London Medium.

Dr. Brown and William Archer (the dramatist) were close friends before the death of the latter, and the spirit of William Archer is said to have spoken to Dr. Brown through the Medium's control, Feda, an Indian maiden, whose characteristics of language will be noted in the following extract from the report:

"William Archer says, 'Yes, I have got a brain,' and he says, 'The brain that I am functioning through now was in some way contained in my'—Oh, dear!—'in my physical body on earth. It was part of it, yet independent of it . . . I think all impressions come through the etheric brain, and they through the physical one, and that is the reason why when the etheric brain is separated by what we call death from the physical brain, the physical brain no longer functions.

"The etheric brain, which was the vital part of the physical brain, is gone, separated, has an independent existence with, he says, 'as much an independent existence as a child has in the ordinary physical process known as birth ... '

" 'He says. 'When the greatest shock of all comes, which is physical death, that of course is the culminating, the great shock to the physical, the etheric brain has to leave; the cord is broken; the connection is broken; it cannot be brought back. It leaves and it draws with it all the component parts of the etheric body. That is the reason the physical body cannot last long without some artificial help, as embalming. Left to itself it collapses. It disintegrates; disintegrates,' he says, 'because the etheric part has been the material part.' He says, 'I must use the word material—it has been the material and essential part of the physical body.

" 'The etheric body dwells in the fluids of the physical body. You understand? It dwells in the water—the fluids of the body partly, and partly it lies outside. That causes—causes—causes that causes the phenomena we hear of as the aura. The etheric body, that which is within the physical partly—it cannot be entirely in, but is a little outside the physical, may reach two or three inches outside—causes this emanation which is perceptible to clairvoyants and is called the aura or the auric emanation. At death we know there is no aura ... '

" 'The Materialist says that because a man's physical brain is destroyed there can be no future life because he has got nothing to work upon. He ignores, because he hasn't proved its existence, the etheric brain. He hasn't located it, therefore he ignores it!' He says, 'We always ignore that which we haven't yet located, but it is there, and we must locate it.' "

According to Professor Brown's account, the ghost of William Archer said much more on this particular subject at the time.

PART TWO

BELIEVED HIMSELF DEAD, FEARED SHOCKING WIFE

When Dr. O. A. Ostby was 22, he entered a theological seminary from which he graduated in due course and was ordained into the ministery. Serving ten years as a divine he finally severed all connection with the church and has since that time been an ardent student of psychical research.

A writer and lecturer, Dr. Ostby is known to many for his book, *An Awakening to the Universe.* He has both experienced and experimented with the phenomenon of the projection of the astral body, and has detailed many of his adventures to this writer.

" . . . The first experience of being out-of-my-body came quite unexpected," he stated, "and occurred in 1904 at my home in Minneapolis, Minnesota. 1 awoke one night in full clear consciousness and found myself standing in front of the bed looking at my own physical body lying beside my wife and baby boy who is now 28 years of age.

"I knew at once that I, my real self, was outside of my body and that I had passed through what is called death. To my consciousness there was no difference in my makeup from being in the body.

"I thought I had died, but that made no difference to me as I was perfectly happy and in fact had a strong desire to remain in this new state of freedom. But just then the thought struck me that it would be a dreadful shock for my wife to awaken in the morning and find my lifeless form beside her, so I determined that I must try to reanimate my physical form again.

"At that moment I felt a *power of will* take possession of me like steam in a boiler wanting to burst from its confinement. When this power reached a certain degree, I noticed the spiritual *myself* was lifted right off the floor, laid horizontally in space,

49

and pushed slowly, inch by inch, into the physical again.

"I could tell when my heart started to beat again and the blood circulate through my veins. Especially peculiar was the feeling when I observed the mind start to function through the material brain again ... Not long after that I acquired the ability to go in and out at will, with no break in consciousness at all ... "

When Dr. Ostby related the foregoing to me in December 1929, he had not read my instructions, published in *The Projection of the Astral Body*, for accomplishing this seeming miracle at will. Since doing so he has stated that his method was precisely that which I termed *Dynamization of Projection*, in the book.

" ... I could lie on my couch," he goes on to say, "and my astral body would go out without ever being conscious of the separation. I would think it was my physical self until I would discover *that* still on the couch. Often I have lain down on the bench at my office and *jumped off* into the astral, turned and looked at my physical self still on the bench.

"Then I would go to the window, see the traffic in the street, hear people talk, pass through matter, see persons near and far away, go downstairs the back way, through the building, up the front way, and enter my body again.

"While *out* one time I wanted to know what time it was and looked at my watch. It was queer that I could see only the rim of the watch and it was impossible to see the dial and hands, try as I would ... "

"On another occasion I was very anxious to see a certain man. I had never seen him in my life nor any photos of him, and according to my conscious knowledge he lived in Chicago, Illinois, where I had his late address. When I left my body a peculiar thing happened. I knew instinctively and instantly that the person I desired to see was now living in California and not Chicago. Where did that super-conscious knowledge come from?

"I had no consciousness of intervening space but found myself in California, found his new bungalow, noted the street corner, went inside, had a good look at the man, learned he was a dope

50

fiend, etc. Later I investigated the matter physically, secured photos both of the man and the bungalow, and found everything to be exactly as I had seen them with my spiritual eyes while out of my body. I also learned later on that the man really was a dope addict."

To those who would proclaim his statements to be nonsensical, Dr. Ostby simply replies: "Laugh, if you care to—laughing is good for the health."

To those who would have it that his experiences were only vivid dreams, he says: "Then our whole conscious life is a mere vivid dream, or a succession of dreams, and nothing more."

FLOATS HORIZONTALLY IN AIR

A communication dated Dec. 17, 1930, from Mr. H—, of Bournemouth, Eng. serves admirably to show that persons can be perfect strangers and reside in entirely different parts of the world, yet implicitly agree upon points regarding this most unbelievable and rare phenomenon. That fact alone is food for thought. The illustrations spoken of by Mr. H—, were those contained in my book The Projection of the Astral Body, showing the route taken by the phantom on exteriorizing; that is, the phantom rising out of the physical, resting horizontally in the air above it, then floating outward, etc. Mr. H—, says:

"I had a bit of a shock today. I was in Boot's Bournemouth, changing my book at their library, when I happened to pick up a copy of your book. I opened it—and, what a shock! It was those illustrations. They astonished me! I could only say to myself: 'That is I—That is I.'

"When I was about twenty years old I began to have an almost nightly experience of *my body coming out of my body*, and going sometimes on long trips. The trips were usually delightful. I have always kept those experiences mostly to myself. I won't go into details here, though I can do so if you ask it.

"My trips continued for many years and I could, *and did make myself float in the air at will*. The floating was exactly as you

51

have pictured it. I would always begin lying horizontally over my body, float outward, then assume an upright position . . . The experiences became more rare and now I very seldom have one. I have not read your book, not even the Preface, it was the amazement—the actual shock—of seeing those marvellously accurate illustrations which prompted this letter."

AWAKENS IN A STRANGE HOUSE

Hundreds can vouch for the trustworthy character of Dr. Kraft. He is a gentleman of honor and repute, world traveler, Doctor of Medicine, and has been a public official in Milwaukee, one of the larger cities of the United States. Dr. Kraft gave me this account orally at his office in the summer of 1929.

He awoke one night to find himself standing in a house which was some distance from his own. He wondered how he came to be there and was astonished to discover that he was garbed in his night suit. His feet were bare. Naturally he was not a little embarrassed, for he thought he was *physically* present.

"I recognized the house and was especially surprised to find that I could see right through its walls and across the street . . . While I saw no one I heard a voice tell me that the owner of the place was at that particular time on the Pacific coast."

He began to examine himself, realizing that there was certainly something wrong with him; but could find nothing, his body seemed quite natural and substantial, and, "it was not until I passed right through the closed door of the room that I really knew that this was not my physical body."

When this thought came to him, the next was that he was dead and while he felt indescribably vigorous and free he was sorry in his mind to think that his wife would find his lifeless body. Immediately then, he found himself moving toward his own home.

"As I did so, I passed through an apartment house and saw the janitor in the cellar. He was yawning!"

The Doctor stated that when he entered his own home he saw his wife sitting up in bed, and stood watching her. An interval later he entered his physical body with a jump.

"By inquiring into the things I experienced I found them to be correct. I was more than surprised when I found out that the man in whose house I first found myself really was on the Pacific coast."

PROJECTS WHILE WRITING

To Adele Wellman, Secretary of the American Society for Psychical Research, I am grateful, for locating for me a comparatively little known experience of the Reverend W. Stainton Moses. The incident was published in the S. P. R. Proceedings, Vol. XI—1895 although it actually took place on Sunday morning, January 25th, 1874. Moses says:

" ... I was sitting at my table in Clifton Road, time 1 p. m. or thereabouts. I had breakfasted late, about 10.30, and had been writing since breakfast ... I have no remembrance of ceasing to write. *The first thing that I remember was standing beside my body and looking at it.* I did not feel surprised, but only curious to know how I got there. *My spirit body seemed to be disengaged and to be leading an independent existence.*

"While I was looking I was conscious of the presence of the Prophet, who stood beside me. He was robed in sapphire blue, and on his head was a coronet with a very bright star in the middle over the brow. The face was what I have seen before—the face of an old man with a long beard and a moustache, deep-set eyes and large massive brow.

"He explained to me that I was out-of-the-body, and told me to follow him. I remember well the oddity of my sensation when I discovered that the wall of the room was no bar to me. We passed on our way without obstacle until I found that we were in the midst of a very beautiful landscape. How we got there I do not know, but I seemed to have changed almost instantaneously the surroundings of earth for the scenery of the spheres.

"A special effort, I imagine, of my guide enabled me to see my body, and after I had resumed spirit vision to the exclusion of bodily vision. The scenery through which I passed was like an earthly landscape, but the air was more translucent, the water more clear and sparkling, the trees greener and more luxuriant.

"I went along without conversation, and noted the ease with which my will carried me along with a peculiar gliding motion. At the end of my journey we came to a simple cottage, very like many I have seen here, and there I found my Grandmother Stainton. She was just as I had remembered her, only clothed in a long pure robe, with a girdle of deep red. Her hair was bound with a simple fillet, and her whole face and figure were idealized and glorified.

"She attempted to address me, but my guide motioned me away and hurried me back. From this point my memory grows fainter and fainter and I recall no more until I found myself sitting in my chair, the pen on the table by my side, and the paper on which I had been writing before me. The ink was very dry, and I was for a time only partially conscious of what I had seen. It all came back by degrees.

"Now at night it is conceivable that I might be drowsy or sleepy, though I know I was not on the occasion . . . This was midday. I certainly did not go to sleep. I had had breakfast and nothing else two hours ago, and the vision was apropos of nothing that was in my thoughts. It was stated by communicating spirits that the occurrence was real, and that my oblivion of the latter part was caused by the necessity of hurrying me back, as the conditions were not good."

VISITS SCENE OF HER HUSBAND'S BOYHOOD

In a lecture at Sydney, before the Australian Society for Psychic Research, published in The Harbinger of Light of April, 1, 1932, Mrs. Lionel Hall spoke in part on astral body phenomenon during sleep and told of her first conscious out-of-the-body trip.

"I would now like to give my first experience of a projection in a conscious state," said Mrs. Hall. "I have had very many dream flights into the beyond but naturally the most interesting are those that occur when one is awake to all that is passing.

"My first experience of this condition occurred some years ago, when I was told by other means that I could 'See.' After a preliminary hesitation I found myself in the air and looking down upon the harbour beneath me. Different vessels were shown to me and other incidents which were verified next day.

"After looking down on the water and on the city, I next found myself moving through the cloud layer, in fact I was completely surrounded by cloud, but finally emerged on the other side in what seemed to be interminable space and unending brightness. Not sunlight that comes in beams, but corpuscular light that is pure white, composed of dots and throws no shadow.

"The feeling in this zone is one of complete tranquility and harmony. Traveling on I then entered into what I may describe as a most beautiful country garden, the wonderful condition of which can scarcely be imagined by anyone who is only familiar with the earth plane. Here, for the first time I met my husband's brother who had passed over some fifteen years previously. He came to meet me and explained that we were on the third sphere.

"He told me that he was now going to show me places where both he and my husband spent their boyhood, just, as he said, to prove his identity. Many things were shown to me and boyish pranks detailed.

"In recounting these to Mr. Hall next day we found that while some of them were remembered, others had been practically forgotten, and only brought to memory by this episode. One incident is worthy of special mention. A man by the name of Mitchell, who was clean shaven when the boys were in the district together, was shown to me with a beard.

"Of course Mr. Hall thought that there had been some mistake, but some four months later, when visiting the district, we stopped on the roadside near some houses, and to Mr. Hall's astonishment

55

this man came out, and he certainly had a large black beard."

PROJECTS TO MISSING DEAD MAN

To thousands of people, Arthur P. Roberts needs no introduction. Called by many, "The Psychic Detective," during his life he has had an uncanny ability for locating lost persons and objects. He was born in Denbigh, Wales, and newspapers of his native land referred to him as 'The Great Welsh Prophet.' He came to America long ago, lived for some time at Fox Lake, later moving to Milwaukee, his present home.

While quite illiterate, Mr. Roberts has solved problems which have baffled most ingenious minds; in fact I do not exaggerate when I say that a large volume would be required to hold the accounts of them all. The Police Departments in numerous cities of the Middlewest contain many records of mysteries which Roberts has solved. He makes no secret of the fact that his extraordinary talent is purely mediumistic and that his feats are accomplished by clairvoyance, clairaudience, and astral body projection. Here is an interesting case:

Some years ago a man named Duncan McGregor of Peshtigo, Wisconsin, disappeared and although police and detectives scoured the country and several large rewards were offered for information concerning his whereabouts, no clues were forthcoming. A few weeks later, Mrs. McGregor, in company with two lady friends consulted Mr. Roberts. He explained to them that they must be absolutely quiet, disconnected the electric doorbell, locked the door, then reclined on a couch in a partially darkened room and concentrated on the problem before him.

So much by way of explanation. I now quote Mr. Roberts: "As near as I can explain it, I tried to forget everything in the universe, except Duncan McGregor and his fate. I said to *myself*, 'I have a difficult task before me and I want *you* to do all you can to assist me'.

"This may sound weird to some, but there was a feeling as if

56

I possessed two distinct individualities and as if one appealed to the other for help. I cannot explain it; I can only describe my sensations. Gradually there came a drowsiness, almost identical with that sensation known as going to sleep—possibly more like being hypnotized.

"As I lay there with every faculty centered on Duncan McGregor—where he was or what had happened to him—I passed into a profound slumber . . . Then I awoke, not as one does when aroused from sleep, but rather as if my senses were slightly numbed.

"My first sensation was of light—a dim, indistinct white light which was not like daylight, nor like any other light I ever saw. It seemed to come from no particular point, and was peculiarly white. It was not strong and made everything seem indistinct. I did not try to take note of any surroundings—only the peculiar light.

"By degrees my perception became more and more open to the fact that I was moving with an even gliding motion, akin to floating. This was without any conscious effort on my part. Then the scene changed and I was in a large room in which were a number of men. It was evident it was night time and instinctively I knew that one of the men present was Duncan McGregor.

"Although I could see the room and everything in it, I did not know where I was. In fact, the thought that I was in the room no more entered my mind than it does the mind of a person in normal condition when he looks at a picture. It was like a picture, except that the individuals talked and moved.

"From the moment I saw McGregor my faculties became keen, the strange numbness passing away. All my senses seemed concentrated on him and his companions, so that but indistinct note was made of other things. I had sent my astral self to see certain things and it seemed that nothing extraneous could now be considered.

"Step by step I accompanied Duncan McGregor to his death that night. When we left the place where I first found him it was dark, yet I could see as plainly as if it were daylight. There was the ordinary gloom of night, yet that mysterious white light was present. This existence of darkness and light simultaneously is most puzzling. I cannot explain it. It has no parallel in the ordinary world and therefore it is difficult to describe or to understand.

" . . . I cannot make public the way in which Duncan McGregor met his death. There are facts regarding it I learned while out of my body, which, if capable of legal proof would result in criminal action being placed against certain individuals. Such testimony as I could give would not be admitted as evidence in court . . . and further it would be revealing affairs of a private nature pertaining to Mrs. McGregor. At the same time I witnessed the scene of Duncan McGregor's death, just as it actually happened more than a month before.

"After witnessing his death, there was a shift of scenes, similar to the change of slides in a stereopticon. I was floating in my ghost body above a river with trees on the bank. An unknown power seemed to direct me to a certain spot on the river. It was a locality I had never visited in the flesh. My control halted me over the water, just opposite a cluster of three trees, and looking down I could see the body of the man I had followed to his death.

"The water was no obstacle to my vision. I felt that I must go down through the water and touch the body and as that thought came to me I felt myself sink into the river and the chill of the water struck me so that I shuddered with the cold.

"Down to where the water-soaked form lay I went, and actually seemed to touch it. It was caught under some logs and driftwood, and I realized that was the reason it did not rise to the surface . . .

"I had finished my task and there was an interval of unconsciousness. When I awoke physically it was nearly 6 o'clock and I had been in trance for about four hours and was weak and exhausted. Mrs. McGregor was still waiting and as gently as I

58

could I informed her that her husband was not alive."

Mr. Roberts advised the widow to withdraw her reward of $1,000 which she had offered for information concerning her husband and assured her that his body would soon be found. He described the spot where, while out of his body, he had located the cadaver; a place perfectly unfamiliar to himself, but from his description, Mrs. McGregor recognized the locality as being on the Menomonee River, a spot she had often seen. And as everyone who read of the case in the newspapers at the time will recall, the body of Duncan McGregor was found in the Menomonee River at the precise place designated by A. P. Roberts.

A MOTHER PROJECTS, FINDS HER BABY WELL

In *Schlaf und Tod*, Vol. 2, Franz Splittgerber has written of a minister's wife who had an unusual experience out-of-the-body. I pass on the case as best I can, having to translate it from the German.

Reverend W—, and his wife went for a trip, leaving their baby at home in care of the minister's sister. On the first night of the trip, the wife had the experience of her spirit leaving her body and floating about in the air. She tells of floating all the way back to her home.

Entering the house, she went to the bedroom, found the cradle, and stood before it. Then she bent down, blessed her baby and repeated a verse from the bible. Having done this she looked up and saw that her sister-in-law was in the room. The sister-in-law also observed Mrs. W—, there in her phantom and on doing so uttered a loud scream.

The scream, according to Mrs. W—, caused her to fly back through the air to her physical body where she awoke, fully convinced of her astral experience and entirely satisfied that all was well with her baby at home.

Sometime later, when the Reverend W—, and his wife returned home from their trip, his sister actually corroborated his

59

wife's statements concerning her out-of-the-body experience. She (the Reverend's sister) told of seeing the phantom of Mrs.W—, standing at the cradle, blessing the baby, uttering the bible verse, etc., on the same night when Mrs. W—, claimed to have done so!

NAVAL CAPTAIN PROJECTS TO WIFE

Captain Sumner E. W. Kittelle tells of leaving his body in a report dated January 19, 1913 and published in, *Life and Action:*

"In April I was for about a month Captain of the gunboat Marietta and was lying alongside the dock in Brooklyn, N. Y. My wife remained at the house in the Navy yard at Boston. One night I returned to the ship, from the city, at about eleven o'clock, went to the cabin and in due time retired to my stateroom and went to sleep in my bunk.

"During sleep *I was conscious that I left my physical body* and traveled with seeming great speed over, but some distance above the ground, to Boston, where I sought my own room and took my accustomed place in bed.

"Here after a while I was conscious that my wife had placed her hand upon my shoulder, and I made a strong effort to turn over and respond to her touch. This effort seemed to cause me to leave the bed and room and return over the same route to New York, at the same speed, and thereupon I reoccupied my bunk on board ship and awoke.

"At once it occurred to me that this must be an *experience,* so I reached out and switched on the electric light and noted the exact time. The next day I wrote to my wife and, without telling her anything about my experience, I asked her if she had noticed anything during the night in question.

"Her reply was that she had strongly felt that I was in bed and had reached out and touched me on the shoulder! So real did it seem to her that she sat up to investigate, and finding nothing, thought, nevertheless, that she would make note of the time, which she did, and the two times, hers and mine, were identical!"

PHYSICIAN WATCHES HIMSELF EXTERIORIZE

The case of Dr. Wilste, of Skiddy, Kansas, is quite well known to older researchers. It was first printed in the *St. Louis, Medical and Surgical Journal*, November, 1889, later in Vol. VIII of the S. P. R. Proceedings and in Myer's, *Human Personality and its Survival.* However, many newcomers into the occult field have never read of this remarkable example of exteriorization of the astral double.

Dr. Wilste, who had been suffering from an unusual disease, felt himself gradually sinking, bade adieu to his friends and family and finally sank into unconsciousness. Those near him presumed he was dead. The village churchbell was tolled. In a short time he recovered consciousness again, "but," he says, "the body and I no longer had any interest in common.

"I looked in astonishment and joy for the first time upon myself, the me, the real Ego, while the *not* me closed in upon all sides like a sepulchre of clay. With all of the interest of a physician, I beheld the wonders of my bodily anatomy, intimately interwoven with which, even tissue for tissue, was I, the living soul of the dead body."

The Doctor heard and felt "the snapping of innumerable cords," then slowly he began to retreat from the feet toward the head, as a rubber cord shortens. Reaching the hips he remembered telling himself that there was no life below his hips and discovered that his whole self had collected into the head from which he finally emerged.

"I floated up and down and laterally, like a soap-bubble attached to the bowl of a pipe, until I at last broke free from the body and fell lightly on the floor, where I slowly rose and expanded to the full stature of a man.

" . . . I seemed to be translucent, of a bluish cast and perfectly naked. With a painful sense of embarrassment I fled toward the partially opened door to escape the eyes of the two ladies whom I was facing, as well as the others . . . but on reaching the door I found myself clothed, and, satisfied on that point, I turned and faced the company."

Next Dr. Wilste tells how he saw two men standing in the doorway and one of them passed his arm directly through Dr. Wilste's spiritual body, "without apparent resistance, and the severed parts closed again without pain, as air re-unites."

Dr. Wilste looked at the man's face to see if he had noticed the contact, but the man only stood and gazed toward the couch.

"I directed my eyes toward the couch also and saw my own dead body. It was lying just as I had taken so much pains to place it, partially on the right side, the feet close together, and the hands clasped across my breast. I was surprised at the paleness of the face."

From the eyes of this astral body, Dr. Wilste saw two women kneeling and weeping. He did not recognize them but nevertheless attempted to gain their attention with the object of comforting them as well as assuring them of their own immortality.

"I bowed to them playfully and saluted with my right hand. I passed about among them also but found they gave me no heed. Then the situation struck me as humorous and I laughed outright. They certainly must have heard that, I thought, but it seemed otherwise, for not one lifted their eyes from my body.

". . . They see only with the eyes of the body," he concluded, "they cannot see spirits. They are watching what they think is I, but they are mistaken. That is not I. This is I and I am as much alive as ever. I turned and passed out of the room . . . I never saw the street more distinctly than I saw it then. I took note of the redness of the soil and of the washes the rain had made."

Looking back through the door, Dr. Wilste saw, "a small cord, like a spider's web, running from my shoulders back to my body and attaching to it at the base of the front of the neck. I was satisfied with the conclusion that by means of that cord I was using the eyes of my body, and, turning, walked down the street."

The Doctor then relates at great length the things he encountered while out-of-his-body, at such length, indeed, that I dare not take the space to reproduce them here but refer the reader to the original account for the complete story.

Walking up a road, facing north, he found that his "memory, judgment, and imagination, the three great faculties of the mind, were intact and active."

He heard an entity speaking to him in a language which, though English, "was so eminently above my power to reproduce that my rendition of it is as far short of the original as any translation of a dead language is weaker than the original."

At a certain place in the road which the Doctor described as marking the boundary between the two worlds, his astral trip came to an end.

" . . . A small dense black cloud appeared in front of me and advanced toward my face. I knew that I was to be stopped. I felt the power to move or to think leaving me. My hands fell powerless to my sides, my shoulders and head dropped forward, the cloud touched my face and I knew no more . . . "

When he regained consciousness he was back in his physical body again on the little white cot at his home and exclaimed in great astonishment: "Must I die again!"

Many things which Dr. Wilste saw during the interval he was thought to be dead—the two gentlemen standing in the doorway; his wife and sister kneeling and weeping; the washes made by the rain—were, after his return to physical life, verified as correct. The corroborative statements of those who were present are recorded in the S. P. R. Proceedings, by Dr. Hodgson.

GOES PROSPECTING IN THE ASTRAL BODY

In a letter dated Feb. 1, 1931, Mr. F. P. Bell, a prospector, formerly of Olympia, Wash. but now living in Los Angeles, Cal. states that for a time he followed some of this writer's projection instructions with the hope of projecting his astral body voluntarily. He was fairly successful in producing repercussions and aviation type dreams, details of which he elaborates upon in his letter, then goes on to say:

"It was hard for me to hold projection in my mind on going to bed, for it kept me busy thinking all day long and part of the night on the best way to save the timber . . . But finally one night came when I had a dream that I was riding in a car over logs, but it was not jolting me. That started me to reasoning, in the dream, just why I was not being jolted, which must have been the cause of my conscious mind starting to function . . . "

"For then I became conscious! I was in my astral body. The first thought that came to me was, now that I am out, I can go where I please. That thought was uppermost in my mind at all times, and at that moment I was elevated to about fifty feet in the air and travelled at about the same speed up through the canyon.

"As I moved through the air it suddenly entered my mind that it would do me no good to see a treasure of any kind unless I could remember the road to it, and I was trying to get the land-marks fixed in my mind when I was drawn back to my body."

What a disappointment for Mr. Bell. Some, who did not have the experience, may say: "This was but a prospector's dream." But the man who *did* have the experience says: "I was out-of-my-body and conscious."

HAS TWO VIVID EXPERIENCES

I have repeatedly pointed out for many years (in this connect-ion, refer back to: Doctrine of Astral Projection) that aviation-like movements of the phantom are typical, if not essential, to the phenomenon. Such phrases as *walking on air, floating in space, lying in the air,* etc., are common descriptive phrases used by those who have exteriorized. Notice how the two separate experiences of M. L. Hymans (recorded by Richet) corroborate and stress this point, and how similar it is in the descriptions given out by many others. M. Hymans tells of being in a

64

dentist's chair, having his teeth worked upon while under an anæsthetic:

" . . . I had a sensation of walking and floating in the air in the room; and to my great surprise I saw the dentist working over my body and his assistant by his side. The scene was vivid. My body was inert. After a few minutes I lost consciousness and awoke in the dentist's chair again, with a clear memory of what I had seen . . . "

M. Hymans states that his next experience took place in a London hotel. He was suffering with heart-weakness when he awoke in the morning. In a short time he fainted and says: "To my great surprise I found myself high up in the room from where, to my terror, I saw my body in the bed, eyes closed. I tried to re-enter my body, but without success and concluded that I was dead. I could not leave the room and felt chained to it, immobilized in the corner where I found myself.

"An hour or two after I heard knockings on the door . . . I could not respond. A little later the hotel porter climbed through the fire escape to the balcony. I saw him enter the room and look anxiously at my figure and then at the door. Soon the manager and others entered and a physician came. I saw him shake his head when he examined my heart. He introduced a spoon between my lips. I lost consciousness and awoke in bed. The experience lasted for at least two hours . . . "

INDIAN GOES TO HAPPY HUNTING GROUND

Major C. Newell, in a book entitled, *Indian Stories*, has set forth an account of spiritual body projection which was related to him by White Thunder, a chief who ruled over a part of Spotted Tail's tribe. The story being of considerable length I relate it here only in an abbreviated form.

White Thunder wrapped his buffalo robe around himself one evening and fell asleep while his squaw was preparing supper. He awoke to the consciousness that two of his own people wearing robes of white—the sign of the Holy Lodge—were there and asking him to follow them.

He called to his squaw to tell her that he would go with the two in white and wondered why she did not answer him. His body felt "as light as air" he explained, as he arose to go to her and although he tried to tell her again she paid no attention.

Just then he saw that he was not in his body! His earthly form was sleeping in the buffalo robes! On examination he concluded that his earthly body was dead and that his new body was his spirit. His squaw could not see nor hear him in his new form and he wondered just what to do.

One of the men in white told him to come along with them and later they would bring him back to live for "many winters" in his material body. He went along. They told him that "the spirit was the life of his former body."

"As we went on and on." White Thunder related, "we lost sight of the earth and in front of me I saw what looked like a great shining river that seemed to extend far up into the sky. I could not see the end of it but the guides said it led to the land of the Great Spirit. All of the people that live on the earth and are good will at last go away on the river . . . The banks of the river were becoming lighter. Soon we approached the shore and saw tepees of my people. Many whom I had known in earth life came to meet me and I was overjoyed to be among my old friends."

On reaching a large wigwam, which White Thunder knew to be that of a Great Spirit, he was told to go back to the earth and tell his friends to treat all men as brothers and to be kind to those who were sick and suffering.

"The guides showed me many strange places on the way back. I saw spirits who were happy and many who were in sorrow. I saw those that had been bad . . . suffering for the evil deeds they had done . . . After a while we were back to earth and the guides in white took me to the place where my people were camped.

"I saw that my wife was sitting beside my body crying and my children were with her calling for their father. When I looked at my flesh-body wrapped in skins, I dreaded to go back into it . . . but the guides said I must. I seemed to fall asleep and when I awoke I was back in my body again. I struggled to get free. My wife cut the cords that bound me and I sat up. They cried for joy to find I had come back again. I arose and had my old heavy body, to carry again."

White Thunder told Major Newell he had been out of his body for "three sleeps" and in the meantime his squaw and children had bound his supposed corpse with cords and taken it to the Missouri River for burial.

PROJECTION DURING ANAESTHESIA

The experience of Mrs.—, of Penns Grove, N. J. is an interesting case of projection while under anæsthesia. She says:

"While in one of the largest hospitals in Pittsburgh, Pa., a few years ago, I was obliged to undergo an operation. It was the first time in my life I was ever given an anæsthetic, and almost immediately after I commenced to breathe in, as instructed, I was overcome with a most perfect sensation of bodily comfort.

"To my surprise I found myself standing in company with the doctors and nurses, and I certainly did notice every detail of my surroundings—my physical body lying limp upon the table, the instruments, bottles, and so forth, and especially the fact that the cap on one of the nurses was out of place.

"Suddenly I looked up through the glass ceiling and beheld my grandmother, who had passed away ten years before. She came right over to me and took me by the hand and told me to come with her quickly as there was but little time. We passed through the glass ceiling of the room as easily as if it had been merely a curtain of smoke.

"When outside in the sunshine, grandmother called my attention to many familiar objects. She even pointed out the roof of my home, which I could distinctly see through the trees. I was

enjoying the wonderful experience very much when grandmother suddenly said: 'It is now time for you to return.'

"Before I had time to object, I awoke on my bed in the hospital,
with the nurse bending over me . . . That is about all I can tell
you about my out-of-the-body experience, except that after
coming out of the ether, my body, especially my hands, seemed
very heavy. The occurrence was very pleasant, and if that is the
way one feels after so-called death, I, for one, will have no fear of
dying."

A CASE RECORDED BY JUNG STILLING

The eminent German Pietist, Johann Heinrich Stilling (known
as Jung Stilling; see Lebensgeschichte) who was a renown author and physician, has reported a most remarkable case of
intentional projection made by a Philadelphia man. According
to the account the Philadelphian was well known and respected,
although he had a reputation of possessing mediumistic powers.

On the occasion in question he was visited by the wife of a sea
Captain. The woman was in sorrow. Her husband had gone on
a voyage to Africa and Europe and had not returned. There had
been no tidings from his vessel which was long overdue.

Hearing the tale of the anxious wife the medium left her and
entered the adjoining room, where he reclined upon his couch
and apparently went to sleep. She waited for a long time and
became greatly alarmed as the moments passed, for the medium
was beginning to show many signs of death.

After a while, however, he awakened. He informed the
nervous woman that *he had made a voyage in his astral body
and had actually visited with her husband* in a coffee-house in
London. He also told her the reasons, which her husband had
given him, for his not having written, adding that he would soon
return to Philadelphia.

When the sea Captain finally did return his wife questioned
him regarding the matter and he corroborated all of the state-

ments of the projector. On being taken into the presence of the medium the husband uttered an exclamation of surprise, saying that he had seen the identical man in the London coffee-house, and that it was the same strange man who had told him how his wife was worrying about him. He further told how he had answered the man and given him the reasons for his failure to return and neglect of writing, and said that after doing so he suddenly lost sight of the stranger entirely.

An unbelievable account indeed! One can scarcely blame the average person if he refuses to believe such, even if recorded by Jung Stilling.

METHODIST LADY PROJECTS, BECOMES MEDIUM

In an article, *How I Discovered My Mediumship*, published in *The Spiritual Pathfinder*, Myrtle E. Larson, Pastor of the *Temple of Spiritual Truth*, Granite City, Illinois, tells a noteworthy experience. Needless to say I have Mrs. Larson's permission to relate the story here, which was given me shortly after she returned from an interesting series of sittings before the New York section of the American Society for Psychic Research.

At the time of the occurrence—December 31, 1919, Mrs. Larson was of the orthodox Methodist faith. In the evening her three year old child, who had been ill, developed a serious fever. Mrs. Larson went to his bed, placed her hand upon his head, closed her eyes, and prayed that the fever would subside.

"After a few moments I felt very strange. I was sure this was the power of God touching me and with every confidence I gave up to the influence. Still with my eyes closed, I felt a floating sensation and soon was met by a seemingly real person appearing to be a little Indian maiden, dressed in Indian robes and arrayed in beads.

"Two beautiful black shiny braids of hair were hanging over her shoulders. She reached her hand for me . I stepped forward and was taken for a long journey which I later learned was an astral flight. Words of earth are inadequate to describe the experience of this journey which was all too short. My hostess spoke, saying: 'You will know me hereafter as Sunflower, an Indian maid who lived on earth 80 years ago. I have many things to tell you as time goes on. I came to this plane at the age of sixteen. I shall never leave you . . . You must return now for you have been away a long time. The baby is well. I'll talk to you again very soon'.

"Slowly I regained consciousness . . . My hand was still on the head of my little son who was now without fever. Two hours had elapsed . . . No doubt there are those who would feel that such an experience would cause alarm or frighten one; but on the contrary it seemed very natural and not at all strange. In addition it brought an understanding and peacefulness never before experienced. All life took on a greater aspect and I seemed to have found myself—a new heaven and a new earth had dawned . . . "

VISITS HER COUSIN'S FUTURE HOME

Mrs. Lenora S. Brewster who lives in a small town in the state of New Hampshire has had many out-of-the-body experiences, most of which have been of the involuntary type, preceded by a numbness of the body and commencing in the half-awake state, usually in the early hours of morning.

When exteriorization is about to take place, Mrs. Brewster explains that she feels as if being caught up in a powerful current of force, and for a short interval there is a snapping pain in her head, which soon passes off, and is replaced by a sensation of delightful lightness.

According to her testimony, Mrs. Brewster has never been able to consciously direct her projected astral body, but has simply *sailed* along wherever carried, being in distress all the while with a painful tightness at the throat, which becomes so unbearable that she is forced to return to the physical body again.

In all her conscious astral excursions she has found herself amid the physical objects of the world of matter, and only once did she ever encounter a disembodied spirit—that of her husband's sister, "in all her natural coloring of earthly life." And while she has never been able to see her physical body while projected from it, she could see her husband very clearly as he lay asleep.

Mrs. Brewster, on one occasion, found herself projected and standing in the parlor of a strange and palatial house, where she took particular notice of the furnishings, and "from the parlor I soared up a great stairway and down a hall into a room where lay an old lady. I approached the bed with some hesitation, although I felt sure of being invisible. Suddenly she awakened, and acted as if she could see me, for she sat up on her elbow and looked straight at me.

"I was much embarrassed at being there in a strange house like a thief. She no doubt thought me a ghost of the dead . . . I began to retreat, going *over,* instead of around the stair-railing, and down—down—down, with an accompanying sinking feeling at the pit of my stomach. Then there was a "zinging" in my ears, and in a moment I was sitting up breathless in my physical body and in my own bed . . . "

What subsequently took place is the most interesting part of Mrs. Brewster's adventure. Two years later she went to Concord —a distance of forty miles from the town in which she lived—to visit her cousin. The latter lived in a house which had recently been purchased, furnishings and all, from the estate of an elderly lady, Miss M—, who had died some time before.

It was the first time she had ever visited the place physically, and Mrs. Brewster goes on to say: " . . . A maid ushered me into the same parlor in which I stood that night in my astral body! Looking about I knew I had seen the place before but could not quite remember until I stepped into the hall, when my cousin came down the stairs to welcome me. I had found the place of my astral adventure!

71

Mrs. Brewster, on this visit to her cousin, also learned that the little old lady, whose bedroom she had haunted in her astral body two years before, was Miss M—, the late owner and occupant of the place. An interesting conjecture is suggested in the idea that Mrs. Brewster's phantom body, appearing in Miss M—'s, sleeping chamber may have been to the latter a harbinger of death; for Miss M— died shortly afterward. But, be that as it may.

"Having looked the house over many times since," continues Mrs. Brewster, "I find the room in which the old lady slept to be in the opposite direction from which it seemed to me that night . . . It was as if I had been looking at it in a mirror when in my astral body . . . "

Mrs. Brewster takes oath that her story is true, and has given me the names of all parties involved. There was even a far more significant aftermath than has here been related, but of too personal a nature for inclusion.

MINISTER FLOATS ABOVE HIS FREEZING BODY

A comparatively well known case of the inner self exteriorizing from its physical counterpart is that of the Rev. L. J. Bertrand, a Huguenot minister, who gave Dr. Hodgson an oral, and Prof. William James, a written account of his unique experience.

Rev. Bertrand with an old guide and a group of students commenced a dangerous ascent of the Titlis, going straight upward, instead of by the long Truebsee Alp trail.

On reaching a high altitude, Rev. Bertrand, who was a little weary from the climb, stopped, and, since he had been on the summit many times before, decided to stay where he was. The remainder of the party could go on, under the conditions that the guide take them up by the left and come down by the right, and that W—, the strongest of the students would keep his place at the rear end of the rope.

Promising to carry out the instructions given them, the party went on their way, leaving Rev. Bertrand who sat down to rest, his lower limbs dangling over a dangerous precipice. Eventually the Rev. put a cigar in his mouth; but as he attempted to light it, a strange feeling came over him. Although the match burned his fingers he could not throw it down! He was freezing to death!

"This is the sleep of the snows," he said to himself. "If I move I'll roll down into the abyss! If I do not I'll be a dead man in thirty minutes."

He started praying, then relinquishing all hope for himself, decided to study the process of freezing to death. His hands and feet became frozen first, finally his head became unbearably cold and he passed out of his physical body.

". . . . . Well, thought I, at last I am what they call a dead man, and here I am — a ball of air in the air, a captive balloon still attached to earth by a kind of elastic string and going up, always up."

On seeing and recognizing his inert physical body below him, "my own envelope," as he called it, he said:

"There is the corpse in which I lived and which I called me — as if the coat were the body, as if the body were the soul — deadly pale, with a yellowish-blue color, holding a cigar in its mouth and a match in its two burned fingers. Well, I hope that you shall never smoke again, dirty rag . . . If I only had a hand and scissors to cut the thread which ties me still to it.

"When my companions return they will look at that and exclaim, 'the Professor is dead.' Poor friends. They do not know that I never was as alive as I now am . . ."

At this point in his experience, the Rev. Bertrand's spiritual sight began to function; that is, he was clairvoyant, from the eyes of his spiritual body.

"I see the guide going up by the right, when he promised me to go up by the left. W——, was to be the last, and he is neither first nor last, but alone, away from the rope.

"Now the guide thinks that I do not see him, because he hides himself behind the young man whilst drinking from my

73

bottle of Madeira. Well, go on, poor man, I hope that my body will never drink of it again. Ah! there he is stealing my leg of chicken. Go on, old fellow, eat the whole chicken if you choose, for I hope my miserable corpse will never eat or drink again."

Rev. Bertrand rose higher and higher in his astral body, or "bubble" as he expressed it and clairvoyantly saw his wife, who was not to arrive until next day, and four other people in a carriage on their way to Lucerne and stopping at the hotel of Lungren; but felt neither joy nor sorrow, and could not be happy because "the thread, though thinner than ever, was not cut."

His astral ascension suddenly turned to a descension and he felt a shock and as if someone were pulling the *balloon* downward, as the guide who had returned, rubbed his stiff physical body with snow.

"When I reached my body again I had a last hope — the balloon seemed much too big for the mouth. Suddenly I uttered an awful roar, like a wild beast; the corpse swallowed the balloon, and Bertrand was Bertrand again."

The guide assured Rev. Bertrand that he had almost frozen to death, to which the latter replied:

"I was less dead than you are now, and the proof is that I saw you going up the Titlis by the right, whilst you promised me you would go by the left. Now show me my bottle of Madeira and we will see if it is full."

The guide, astonished, knowing it would be physically impossible for his Captain to have seen through the mountain, fell down and stammered.

"You may fall down and stare at me as much as you please," Rev. Bertrand added, "but you cannot prove that my chicken has two legs, because you stole one of them."

The good Reverend forgave his followers for their disobedience and when they reached the inn, the guide told everyone at the place that the Captain must surely be the devil himself.

Later, when the party arrived back in Lucerne, they found Mrs. Bertrand already there.

"Were there five of you in the carriage and did you stop at the Lungren Hotel?" inquired the Reverénd.

"Yes!" replied his wife. "But who told you!"

OVER THE HOSPITAL BED

On August 13, 1930, Miss M. A. B. of Letchworth Hertford-shire, wrote me, saying:

"I once had to undergo a slight operation, for which purpose ether was administered, at a large hospital in Northern Eng-land. I had recently lost a brother; and almost at once I had the strong idea 'this is what brother felt like when he died. I won't die — I won't.

"I struggled violently, so that two nurses and the specialist were unable to hold me, and were obliged to hurry for chloro-form and try that . . . The next thing I knew there was some piercing screaming going on, *that I was up in the air and look-ing down upon the bed over which the nurses and doctor were bending.*

". . . What specially struck me, and remains particularly vivid in my mind, was the white crosses on the nurses' backs, where the bands of their white uniforms crosses in the back. I was aware that they were trying in vain to stop the screaming, in fact I heard them say: 'Miss B—, Miss B—, don't scream like this. You are frightening the other patients.'

"At the same time, I knew very well that I was quite apart from my screaming body, that I could do nothing to stop. I said to myself: 'Those silly idiots, if they but had enough sense to send for E——, a great friend of mine waiting below in the hospital, I know she could stop it.'

"And just then the strangest thing happened. At my thought, that was exactly what they did! One of the nurses rushed downstairs and begged her to come up. She touched my physical body by the hand, spoke to me, and immediately the screaming ceased . . . In a short time I was physically conscious again . . ."

FINDS HER DOG IN ASTRAL WORLD

Of particular interest to animal lovers and those who wonder if their pets survive death is this communication by Winifred Hunt from the Occult Review of March 1930:

". . . Early last June, my greatly loved fox terrior passed away at the advanced age of sixteen years. Three days after the occurrence at about daybreak, as I lay in my bed awake, I suddenly found myself outside of my body. All else was quite normal — the room, the bed, my physical body lying upon it; yet I, myself, was a thing apart, and in that brief moment of freedom and liberation my emotions were difficult to analyze. I seemed to be suspended between the floor and ceiling!

"I remember distinctly of looking down upon my physical body—but my joy was complete when into my arms sprang my little dog, young and full of life. He seemed to be overjoyed at finding me and we clung together, I caressing him and actually conscious of the smooth warm softness of his head and coat. Like all who love animals and who have been honored by a dog's love and devotion, I knew intimately all his little ways. It seemed natural to be out of my body and with my dog.

"Suddenly I felt a swift rushing impulse, a descent like lightning, and in a flash I realized that I was going back to my physical body and that my dog could not accompany me. Violent anger and resentment filled my whole being. I mentally resisted and set my entire will power in opposition to the force that would separate me from happiness . . . I came back with a fearful jerk, and sitting up I actually heard my dog's voice close to me.

"I felt utterly exhausted . . . The comfort, the knowledge that my dog lives and loves me, has brought into my life, is

76

something that I am glad and thankful to hand on to all who have loved and lost their pets."

In this connection it is interesting to note that years ago M. Ernest Bazzano collected 69 cases where dogs, cats, horses, etc. were chief actors in diverse spirit manifestations.

EXPERIENCES OF GLADYS OSBORNE LEONARD

In a recent and most remarkable book, *My Life in Two Worlds* (Cassell & Co., Ltd. London) the renowned medium, Gladys Osborne Leonard, whom Sir Oliver Lodge has designated as one of the best he has ever known, tells of her first experience in leaving the physical body. She was lying down one day, when suddenly she had a feeling, described as pleasant, that her body was not making actual contact with the bed.

". . . What happened I shall never forget; it was wonderful. I did not move consciously in any way, either limb or muscle, and my eyes were closed. I wondered how far my body might be above the bed, and by a little mental effort I opened my eyes and looked down and saw my physical body resting on the bed, and I, in my astral body, seemed to be resting above it.

"To show you how clear my thoughts were, I noticed that the head of my physical body was lying on a particular night-dress case with an embroidered corner. I was surprised at seeing it there, because I was not aware of its having been changed that morning for the one I had been using.

". . . The next thing I felt was that my astral body was getting farther and farther away from my physical body, and I seemed to be hovering over the edge of the bed for a few seconds. Then I began to feel just a little nervous, and the thought flashed across my mind; *Shall I be able to get back easily?* That question and my slight fear drew me back about a foot toward my physical body. But my interest got the better of my fear, and I thought: *Whatever happens, let me go through with it.*

"The moment I so determined I became aware of my husband opening our flat door, which makes a slight noise on being opened, and speaking to someone in the hall outside. He was speaking in a low voice so as not to disturb me. I thought, I should like to go and see to whom he is speaking, and I don't know how it happened, but I found myself at once, standing by my husband's elbow at the flat door.

"I was not aware of passing through the bedroom door, which is kept closed, but there I was . . . I saw the man he was talking to was from the gas company. What they were talking about I did not notice, because, just after I joined them (in my astral body) a maid from one of the upstairs flats passed them, and I saw my husband, without speaking to her, take a coin from his pocket and hand it to her."

Several further episodes in her experience followed and at last Mrs. Leonard found herself lying just above her physical form again, fearing she would not be able to re-enter it. She goes on to say:

"My astral felt quivery, and the feeling came to me — there is going to be difficulty about it. Then I told myself, there won't be any difficulty if you keep calm about it, you will slip back. I thought that, or made myself think it. I seemed to slip lower and lower, yet not thinking again so connectedly as before, when suddenly I found I was resting on the bed again. I dug my elbow into the bed and felt it solid, which made me realize that I was back in the physical."

The adventure being over, a check-up was made which revealed that the incidents which she witnessed astrally — the man from the gas company, the maid, the embroidered nightgown case, etc., were correct.

At another time Mrs. Leonard claims to have made a trip in her subtle body and visited with the spirit of a man who had taken his own life. A few days later Sir Walter Gibbons called upon her, looking very tired and exhausted.

"I asked him what was the matter. He replied, 'I have had an awful time on the astral plane during sleep. The night before last I was taken to the plane where the suicides go, and there I saw my old friend who killed himself the previous day because he had got so terribly into debt and financial trouble.'

"Wait a minute, I said, I think I have been there too; wait till I describe it to you. I did so, and alternately Sir Walter and I described details of the place to each other, until we were certain we actually had been to the same place, and seen the same man."

GOES DOWNSTAIRS IN GHOST BODY

Several accounts were given me by an educated lady of Glouchester, England, an artist and F.R.H.S. Miss P——, I shall have to call her for she requests that her name be withheld from publication and states that she is not actively interested in either Spiritualism or Theosophy and is not associated with any occult order. Miss P——, by chance, read some of my writings on the subject of projection, and wrote to me, relating several instances in which she found herself out of her body and conscious. I here pass on one which took place at her home in 1929:

"...I had written a letter one evening and given it to my brother to post in the morning, in case I should not be down before he went out. He put the letter on the hall table where I saw it as I went upstairs to bed. Before I went to sleep I thought of something in the letter I wished I had not said and decided *not* to send it, but to get up real early and go down and get it before my brother took it to post.

"I could have gone down then but was afraid I might disturb my people, and besides I was rather afraid to go through the dark hall. The house seems so eerie I am always afraid to walk about through it in the dark. So I went to sleep.

"The next thing I knew I was half way down the bottom flight of stairs in a ghost body! I was looking for the letter, but I do not know how I got there. I was as conscious as I am right now. It was not at all like a dream.

79

"The hall was dreary save for a shaft of moonlight coming in through the glass over the front door and I noticed everything as I went on, even the pattern of the stair carpet. I went to the hall table. The letter was not there . . ."

"Miss P——, then tells how she made a search for the missing letter but was unable to find it. Becoming somewhat frightened at her own peculiar actions she started back up to her sleeping room again, but knew no more after she reached the middle of the first flight of stairs—the exact spot where she first became conscious in her ghostly body — and momentarily found herself physically awake in her bed, fully aware of what had taken place.

". . . Next morning I was up early and went down stairs before brother arose. Looking upon the hall table I found the letter was *not* there. I asked brother where it was and he said he had taken it from the hall table and put it elsewhere the night before. When I told him of my experience he said I must have been dreaming or walking in my sleep . . ."

And isn't that what most people would say? But Miss P——, revolts at such an explanation by saying:

"How could I be dreaming when I was conscious? How could I be walking in my sleep when I was awake?"

WALKS ON AIR, SEES PHYSICAL BODY

The reputable theologian, publisher, and writer, Dr. I. K. Funk related a case of astral projection in his book, *Psychic Riddle.* The subject described how he lost control of his body by reason of a cold numbness which advanced over it. This loss of control and numbness overcame him on a number of occasions before he actually left his body.

". . . There came a flashing of lights in my eyes and a ringing in my ears, and it seemed for an instant as though I had become unconscious. When I came out of this state I seemed to be walking on air. No words can describe the exhilaration and freedom that I experienced. No words can describe the clearness of mental vision. At no time in my life had my mind been so clear and so free ... I became conscious of being in a room and looking down on a body propt-up in bed, which I recognized as my own. I cannot tell what strange feelings came over me! This body, to all intents and purposes, looked to be dead.

"There was no indication of life about it, and yet here I was, apart from the body, with my mind thoroughly clear and alert, and the consciousness of another body to which matter of any kind offered no resistance ... After what might have been a minute or two, looking at the body, I began to try and control it, and in a very short time all sense of separation from the physical body ceased, and I was only conscious of a direct effort toward its use. After what seemed to be quite a long time, I was able to move, got up from the bed, dressed myself, and went down to breakfast ... "

In answer to the criticism invariably advanced — that this was merely a 'vivid dream' — the subject says:

"I know that many people may think that the statements recorded here are simply the result of an active imagination, or perhaps a dream, but they are neither the one nor the other. If the whole world were to rise up ... it would not make one particle of difference in my mind, as I am absolutely certain that I have been as free from my physical body as I ever will be, and that my life apart from it was far more wonderful than any life I have ever experienced in it ..."

SEES HIMSELF SEPARATE DURING ANAESTHESIA

The widely known American writer and philosopher James A. Edgerton has presented me with a copy of his absorbing book, *Invading the Invisible*, and has given me permission to quote the out of the body experience of his son.* The son, James

---

*Years ago Mr. Edgerton discovered that *time* is the fourth dimension, that it meets all mathematical requirements and that the hypothesis is metaphysically valid. This was before Minkowsky. The findings were syndicated in a number of American newspapers.

C. Edgerton, who is well known in aviation circles and who never had a previous psychic experience, tells the story in his own words:

"This experience, which absolutely convinces me of a future personal life, was produced by an anaesthetic in preparation for an operation for appendicitis. There was no conscious background for the experience as it was totally dissimilar from any with which I am familiar.

"In the first place let me say that I was in full possession of my faculties, as there was no fever or other mental deterrent present. As is usual I was strapped to the operating table and was given an anaesthetic through a face mask which completely obscured vision. I was fully conscious of inhaling three full breaths.

"On the second breath, however, an unusual train of circumstances started which can best be described by the statement that my physical senses seemed suddenly to shift into a body other than the physical. With no mental lapse whatsoever, I was clearly conscious that I was half sitting up and that my eyes seemed to take on X-ray qualities which reduced my physical body to a mere shadow with the ankle and knee joints slightly more prominent.

"I saw another body within this shell, glistening brilliantly, and as I watched this new body of which I seemed to be a part, and which was more objective to me than my physical body had ever been I slid out of my fleshy envelope with rapidly increasing acceleration. During this interval my other senses were also functioning, the sense of feeling being concerned with a soul shaking wrench which seemed to extend to every cell of my body.

"To my ears came a beautiful sine wave note, corresponding to middle E on the piano, which increased from zero to volume which seemed to fill the universe. Following this I heard a voice which I seemed to respond to as to any physical voice, which repeated these words: 'You are now suffering all the pangs of violent death. You are in the hands of friends and everything will be all right.' I did not lose consciousness until I was entirely separate from the physical body, which I knew beyond any question I had left."

PROJECTS AND APPEARS AT SEANCE

According to the statements of Mrs. L—, of Wanganui, New Zealand, she has had unintentional conscious projections for years, but it was not until she read some of the present writer's works that the thought ever entered her mind that the phenomenon could be produced at will. Mrs. L—, has since written me of her successes, but at such great length that I cannot detail them.

However, one little experiment—the first she ever tried, is curious. Some of her friends were holding a seance on the night of April 10, 1929 at considerable distance.

" . . . I decided to make an experiment. Being ill and confined to bed in my home, I could not join them at their circle. Knowing the time they would sit would be between 7:30 and 9:30 o'clock, I proposed to myself to project my astral body to their presence.

"Originally I thought as this was but a preliminary experiment I would just try to show myself to them; but later the thought came to me that if I could do that it might be possible to speak to them.

"I must say here that no other person knew of my proposed experiment . . . "

Mrs. L.—, states that being ill in bed she commenced early that evening and made every effort to project her voice as well as her subtle body to the sitters, falling asleep about eight o'clock. When she awoke next morning she was not aware that anything unusual had taken place; but later those who were present at the circle called and expressed great surprise that her form—

even to the nightgown and jewelery on her wrist—appeared at the seance, spoke to them, and vanished. Mrs. L—, can furnish the names of all parties involved in this incident.

As stated, that was Mrs. L—'s, first experiment. She tells of having *conscious* projections also. Once she felt her body going out and it went straight upward "as one might feel if he were drawn directly upward through a tube by hydraulic pressure" and met with things which were utterly beyond earthly words to describe. Mrs. L—, has since informed me that she intends to publish this particular experience in book form in the near future.

On another occasion, the return to her body, after a projection contains some notable points:

" . . . I distinctly remember (on my return) someone, who sounded like myself, saying, 'there is your body—now get back into it' and as I heard the voice say that I looked down and saw my own physical body. It was in the same position it had been in when I went to sleep. The next thing I knew I was going back into it, somewhere about the middle, rather higher than the waist, near the chest . . . "

GHOST GOES HOME DURING OPERATION

Through the kind permission of Mr. Daniel K. Wheeler, past editor of Ghost Stories Magazine, who, a few years ago became greatly interested in my researches into projection phenomenon, the two cases which immediately followed are reproduced from letters to the editor of that periodical. Case one is by a Dallas Texas lady who says:

"I had been sick for about two years and an operation was absolutely necessary . . . My mother could not stand to see me operated on, and so my brother came to the hospital and stayed with me through it all. Just before I went under the ether I told them not to worry about me because I would come out all right . . . I lost consciousness under the ether—and then, suddenly, I found myself walking up Bryan street toward my home.

"I came to our house and went inside. Mother was sitting there hunched up in a chair with tears in her eyes and she turned her face toward me.

"Mamma," I said, "I am so cold. I want to warm myself."

"Then I realized there were other people with me. I saw my baby brother who had died at birth and my mother's mother too. I kept saying over and over: 'I am so cold.'"

The subject next states that she was told to go back to her body, that it was time for her to return, which she eventually did and woke up again in the hospital.

FINDS FREEDOM AND BEAUTY IN SPIRIT WORLD

In case two from Ghost Stories a daughter tells of a projection which her mother experienced and later wrote down. The mother's written account follows:

"... I am writing this experience so that when the time comes for the separation here for any of our loved ones, may this sacred experience come as a sweet benediction to those left just a little while longer ... "

"Gradually the pain which had come upon me grew duller, the voices in my sick room fainter. Then it seemed to me that one after another of those attending me left the room, the last one taking the lighted lamp with her. I was left in darkness and alone. I could not understand why they would all leave me so, and I so desperately ill."

It appears that the subject was presumed dead when those attending her left the room. The account continues:

"Almost immediately a mellow light near the ceiling of my room revealed a company of several apparently very happy people performing duties which they seemed to love to do because of the love back of the duty. Not one appeared troubled or hurried in any way.

"As I gazed in wonderment, I recognized but one, my father who had left us just fifteen years before. He was the only one who seemed to recognize me. He looked from his work once or

85

twice in the direction in which I lay. Finally he approached me so very tenderly that I thought that he had come to take me away. Then I seemed to rise out of matter, into spirit and found myself in the arms of omnipotent love that bore me with my father to a spot whose loveliness mortals cannot describe.

"As we were borne along I seemed to be so free. These are the thoughts which revealed my freedom: 'I have no home—heaven is my home. I have no children—we are all God's children. I have no husband for there is no marrying or giving in marriage here, we are all brothers and sisters and God is our father. I have no cares—God cares for all. Oh!-How free! No cares!' No language here can convey the spiritual meaning of freedom; neither can spiritual freedom be comprehended in the flesh.

"Presently my father paused and made me comfortable in a bower of fragrant flowers and resumed his duties. I seemed to sleep for a while. When I awoke there was a great concourse of people passing to and fro communicating in a language unknown to me. Each one seemed inspired by love in a joy and freedom as each went about his several duties. As an infant is here, I was there, happy in my helplessness.

"Then my father bent over me and lifted me again into his arms. Though not a word had been spoken, I understood the meaning of his action. 'Oh, papa, must I go back to that old body? Can't I stay here? Here I am so happy, so free.'

"With a gentle wave of his hand which I knew meant listen: with his head turned to one side as if to catch the sound of a far off voice, he stood silent, not a sound fell on my ears. When he received his answer he spoke for the first time. He said: 'No child, the Master says that you must return. Your work is not finished.'

"At the Master's command, I was perfectly willing to obey We descended to the earth plane as quietly as we had ascended. passing through every material object. When my father left me. I do not know, *but I do remember looking upon my body as it lay there on the bed.*"

"Then I heard the sound of one of my small daughter's voice calling, 'Mamma—Mamma.' I struggled to get my breath. My husband was bending over me begging me to speak. It seemed hours before I could get warm. My feet and hands were drawn out of shape and almost rigid. . . . It was a long time before I could relate my experience . . . "

BETWEEN TIME AND ETERNITY

In 1932 I had the honor of receiving a letter from J. M. Stuart-Young, the extraordinary novelist, poet, and philosopher, of Nigeria, West South Africa. Stuart-Young who writes under the pseudonym "Odezikau" is the author of belles-lettres, novels, essays, poems, etc., covering a wide range of subjects, e. g., Nigerian Nonsense, Day Dreams of an Exile, Johnny Jones, Guttersnipe and many others.

Having established his identity, I wish to say that Stuart-Young once had a sort of disassociation experience, and has since been experimenting with and studying a subject (Dreaming True) closely related to projection of the astral body.

In the letter he wrote: "Oh! How amazing! I have just read your book and we are both on the same trail . . . My first experience of this kind came about through the taking of an overdose of arsenic and quinine in 1923 . . . I now know what was binding me to my body . . . I gave a brief account of my experience in The Two Worlds shortly after it happened; but I do not now possess a copy of same . . . It seems that you have been succeeding where I have only been fumbling (though at times with amazing accuracy) . . . I am all athrill as I write you, realizing that you, living thousands of miles away, have confirmed my experience . . . "

Through the courtesy of Mr. Oaten, editor of The Two Worlds, I reproduce, from the original, a few paragraphs of Stuart-Young's borderline experience which appeared August 8, 1924. The bulk of the experience relates to the subject's sense of *time*

87

during anæsthesia, so for obvious reasons I omit that. The author says:

" . . . I can cap this phenomenon by my personal experience during my present sojourn in the tropics . . . I was instructed by my doctor to cease taking quinine in small quantities at daily intervals. He supplied me instead with a concentrated liquid. I had to absorb the prescribed dose whenever I felt an attack of fever coming on.

"On the occasion to which I am alluding I fear that I must have drunk too much. After the lapse of half an hour I became violently sick . . . I found myself stone deaf and partially blind. Fortunately my negro servant was available. It happened to be late evening of Saturday, and I had meant to rest over the Sabbath. I was now so prostrate that I reeled like a drunken man . . . The deafness, coupled with the dimness of sight, gave me a strong impression that my body did not belong to me.

"Hayford, the negro steward, had to remain by my bed all night, tending me, wiping away the perspiration from my entire body and massaging my benumbed limbs . . . There were periods when I conceived that I was on the point of dissolution, for *I seemed to be hovering outside my body*, and to envisage the open verandah, where I work and sleep—just as one beholds a scene on the stage. It was something *apart*, something in which I was not an actor.

"There was, moreover, a periodic sensation which I recall very vividly: 'If someone whom I know to be dead comes to me, then I shall realize that I am likewise dead. I will then unhestitatingly break the thread that appears to be holding me to life.' This did not happen. I was quite alone in a realm of mental abstractions.

"Yet the night passed like a breath. I remember starting conversations with my servant . . . He informs me now that I would commence a sentence, wait a matter of two or three minutes, conclude it, and then be silent for nearly an hour, then resume the same conversation. I was dictating to him quite reasonable instructions about my affairs in case I died.

" . . . There is a temporary severance of the consciousness from the brain . . . This severance brings about spells of ignorance—something comparable only to oblivion. It is as though the spirit believed itself to be following a straight road and walking without ceasing. To the observer, however, that progress is impeded by the spirit's casual stopping to observe the marks on the milestones which are passed. In this manner, hours, days, months, even years, may cease to count. For the spirit is standing outside *time*. It only functions in *time* when it has a brain through which to make its presence known. . . . I may say that my confidence in the continuity of life has been greatly strengthened by this accidental incident. There was nothing whatever in the act of "passing" of which to be afraid . . . "

Stuart-Young in one of his latest books, *Dreaming True* (Daniels) says: " . . . My earliest experiences of being wholly and consciously projected carried with them the thought: 'If I now desire to die, I can do so!' Looking down at what seemed my lifeless physical shell was so amazing a sensation that I could scarcely believe at first but that I was the subject of hallucination . . . "

PROJECTION PRECEDED BY CATALEPSY

In a letter dated May 5, 1936, Mr. Bert Bradbury who resides at Knaresboro', Yorks, Eng. states that he has had several unusual psychic experiences, including suspension of physical motivity while conscious, dreams which later "came true" and the seeing of scenes behind him exactly as if they were being reflected in a mirror placed in front of him.

" . . . I had a strange experience during the war," says Mr. Bradbury. "I was senior fireman in the fire brigade in one of the large filling factories in the North of England. I was on night duty and, during the hour of luncheon, I decided to have a short nap.

89

" . . . On awakening I found that I could not move! I seemed to be in a cataleptic state, but was perfectly conscious. Panic seized my mind. What if a fire occurred? I could not sound the alarm! Although the buzzer was within reach, I was powerless to touch it.

"I struggled hard to move. Suddenly I seemed to disengage from my physical self and found myself in the air looking down upon my body . . . Next I had a fear of being certified as dead and of being buried alive. This out-of-the-body state lasted for a short time; after a while I managed to regain the use of my physical self again and I was very thankful.

" . . . May I add that my wife has seen the form of myself enter the kitchen and she almost fainted. Another time she awoke and saw what she recognized as my form entering the bedroom and looking down she found that I was asleep. I have also had others tell me that they have seen me while projected . . . "

BETWEEN TWO WORLDS

The name Gail Hamilton lives immortally among famous American writer. She was also prominent in social affairs at the United States Capitol, and a close relative of James G. Blaine, probably the most conspicuous national figure of the time.

Miss Hamilton tells how she fell into a prolonged state of suspended animation (apparent death) and found herself separated and outside of her physical body. This experience was related by Miss Hamilton in a letter written to her pastor, May 10, 1895. The same letter was later reproduced in a now out of print volume entitled, "Gail Hamilton's Life in Letters," edited by H. Augusta Dodge, published in Boston in 1901. Miss Hamilton wrote her pastor as follows:

"It was early morning, but so swiftly the darkness fell that I have always thought of it as evening. I was standing by my lounge in my room when I felt myself sinking. There was no pain, no alarm, no fear, no feeling. I had but one thought—that it would be a shock to the family to find me on the floor, and that I must get upon the lounge.

"When, or, if I gave up the struggle I do not remember, or the lapse of time, only there was a lapse, and then I heard a voice at the door asking: 'Is everything all right'? I answered: 'No, it is not all right.'

"Unlock the door and let me in."

"I cannot, I am on the floor and cannot get up."

"Another lapse of time and then familiar voices were all around me. I saw nothing, but I seemed to hear everything—lamentations that I had fallen and hurt myself. I told them that I had not fallen but let myself down.

"Much of the time immediately succeeding I was in a passage-way between two rooms. The room on one side was this world, on the other, the next world. The doors of both were closed.

"Once I asked: 'Am I supposed to be alive still?'

"So many friends were around me who had gone out of this world that it suddenly occurred to me whether I myself might not be already gone, and I was about to ask: 'Am I dead or alive?' But I thought if it should turn out that I was still alive the question might sound rather brusque and harsh, and I deliberately softened it to: 'Am I supposed to be living still?'

"To myself it seemed, and it seems still, as if my spirit were partially detached from my body—not absolutely free from it, but floating about, receiving impressions with great readiness, but not with entire accuracy, as if the spirit were made to receive impressions through the bodily organs, and without them could not rely implicitly upon its own observations ... "

It appears that Miss Hamilton's body was removed from Washington, to her home, miles away, while in this state of suspended animation. She goes on to say:

"Of leaving Washington, of the long journey by ambulance and car, I have no knowledge. I seemed to be in a steamboat on the Amazon river, near its mouth. It was only as I neared home that the idea of locality adjusted itself ... When the train stopped, dear familiar faces were all around me—who received me as something consecrated, and held out to me their kind, strong arms . . .

"I had not expected otherwise but I was immeasurably encouraged and strengthened."

Miss Hamilton gives no description of her repossession of physical faculties and the last paragraph of her letter is difficult to understand. She says:

"Under the best professional care, phantoms of the other world disappeared . . . and I slept in a green shaded meadow on a bank of blue flowers, by cool waters in the midst of cresses and rushes and all green growing things."

From all accounts, however, Miss Hamilton seemed none the worse for her sojourn in the other world.

FINDS HER ASTRAL BODY BEAUTIFUL

In the past I carried on extensive correspondence with Caroline D. Larsen, of Burlington, Vermont, relative to projecting the astral body. A short time ago, Mrs. Larsen, whose husband is a noted musician, published a volume, *My Travels in the Spirit World*, which contains much valuable information and many fascinating accounts taken from her own experience, one of which I reproduce here. For a full account of *all* of Mrs. Larsen's spirit world travels, I refer my readers to the book mentioned.

Mrs. Larsen retired one evening quite early and was lying passive, enjoying the music of her husband's string quartet (downstairs) which was rehearsing for a concert, when suddenly the process of exteriorization set in.

" . . . A feeling of deep oppression and apprehension came over me, not unlike that which precedes a fainting spell. I braced myself against it, but to no avail. The overpowering oppression deepened and soon numbness crept over me until every muscle became paralyzed. In this condition I remained for some time. My mind, however, was still working as clearly as ever . . . The next thing I knew was that I, I myself, was standing on the floor beside my bed looking down attentively at my own physical body lying in it.

"I recognized every line in the familiar face, pale and still as in death, the features drawn, the eyes tightly closed and the mouth partly open. The arms and hands rested limp and lifeless beside the body. I gazed at that material form of mine for a few minutes while mingled feelings passed over me. Strangely enough, they were not feelings of great surprise. I experienced no shock at finding myself in this peculiar position. It was chiefly curiosity that possessed my mind. I was perfectly calm and composed as I viewed that mortal form I had just previously inhabited.

"I now raised my eyes from my body and looked around the room. Everything appeared to me as natural as ever. There was the little table with books and trinkets on it. There was the dresser, the armchair, the smaller chairs, the green carpet on the floor ... The music from downstairs kept floating up to my ears. I glanced once more at my body which, to all appearances seemed dead. Then I turned and walked slowly towards the door, passed through it and into a hall that led to the bathroom.

"As I walked toward that room past the stairway, I heard the music coming up with increased force, and I delighted in the lovely adagio from Beethoven's Op. 127 Quartet, a special favorite of mine. As I entered the bathroom the strains gradually diminishing in volume. I now approached a large mirror hanging above the bathroom washbowl. Through force of habit I went through the motions of turning on the electric light, which, of course, I did not actually turn on. But there was no need for illumination, for, from my body and face emanated a strong whitish light that lighted up the room brilliantly."

Mrs. Larsen states that on gazing into the mirror she saw herself, not as a middle-aged woman, but as she was when a girl of eighteen. Her hair was no longer grey but dark brown and wavey and "to my delight I was dressed in the loveliest white

93

shining garment imaginable—a sleeveless one-piece dress, cut low at the neck and reaching almost to my ankles . . . My joy and enthusiasm were unbounded at seeing myself so beautiful . . . It was also an exhilarating sensation to be conscious of the fact that I was outside of my physical body . . . "

Mrs. Larsen continues: "Suddenly I heard the strains of Mendelssohn's Violin Concerto. I knew at once that the Frenchman was playing the solo. It was a habit of his while the music was being changed on the stand. But, as always, he played it out of tune . . . I felt disgusted for the moment, forgetting all about myself and muttered angrily: 'Oh, I wish my husband would tell that Frenchman to play that Concerto in tune or not play it at all.' Fortunately the quartet now began to play again and the soothing music of Beethoven calmed me . . . "

Delighted with the beauty of her astral body, Mrs. Larsen goes on to say: "A block away from us lived Miss B., a friend who had often complimented me on my taste in dressing and on my general appearance. I conceived the notion that I would go to her and show myself. 'Won't she be astonished?' I asked myself. 'If she complimented me before, what will she say now? But first I will go down and present myself to my husband and the other men.'

" . . . I did not fancy that had I succeeded in getting up to Miss B., or down to my husband and the musicians, none of them would have been able to see me . . . Just as I came to a little platform which divides the stairway into two flights, I saw, standing before me, a woman spirit in shining clothes with arms outstretched and with forefinger pointing upwards. There was a look of strong determination on her face as she spoke to me sternly: 'Where are you going? Go back to your body!'

" . . . I knew instinctively that from that spirits command and authority there was no appeal. I must obey. Reluctantly I turned, ascended the stairs, walked through the hall, into my bedroom and up to my bed. My physical body lay there as still and lifeless as when I left it. I viewed it with disappointment . . . In another instant I had again joined with that physical form.

" . . . When I related to my husband the story of my super-natural experience and we compared notes as to what had occurred downstairs, that which I had heard with my astral ears agreed to the smallest detail with what he told me had taken place at the rehearsal . . . "

CONSCIOUSLY DRAWN OUT OF HER FLESH

It is with regret that I cannot here set forth all of the extra-ordinary experiences relating to exteriorization of consciousness which Miss Cromwell Addison has undergone. Miss Addison, who lives at 11 Woodbury Grove, Finsbury Park, N. 4. England, has gone into lengthy detail in furnishing me with accounts of her adventures, and, in my next volume of this series I hope to relate more of them. The following is one of the more brief and simple of her cases:

" . . . One night I awoke to find myself floating over my body, a few feet from the ceiling and could see my physical body on the bed beneath me. I appeared to be in an utterly cataleptic state, yet my consciousness was greatly intensified.

"This was not my first projection as I had several times been observed by others, in the astral body, many miles away; but this time I awakened while yet over my body. Panic seized me as I realized what had occurred and I wondered how to get back before anyone discovered my 'corpse' and this fear instantly made me recoil into my form with a great shock. I lay with mighty pulsations passing through my frame, the very bed appeared to be shaking.

"For a few moments I rested quietly, thinking it over and blaming myself for my fear for I realized the value of the ex-perience I might have had. Presently the vibrations again in-creased in intensity, and a rocking movement ensued. I admon-ished myself to lie still, knowing that if I did not consciously resist there was no cause for fear. By an effort I forced myself to deliberate calmness, waiting for what might still occur.

95

"Presently I was rewarded by a very slow but strong " pulling" sensation at the top of my head, as if from a giant hand. Then, as I remained passive, I was gradually drawn as if out of a tight rubber bathing suit, which I knew to be my flesh. Fully conscious, though in a perfectly cataleptic condition, I mentally commented, 'I am in my bedroom at such and such an address; C— A— is my name; my bed is head to the wall adjoining the garden; now my head and shoulders are passing through the wall; now they are over the garden; now I am out to my knees, and still I could feel the tightness of the flesh below the points which were not free. 'There now I am out to my ankles; what is going to happen?'

"Then I heard words, apparently spoken close beside me: 'Let her return now slowly, and next time she will not be afraid.' The whole process was then gently repeated in the reverse, and I glided into my body as slowly as I had withdrawn. There was a moment of darkness as the head of my astral body slipped into the material form, but not the slightest shock. It was as if the light had been obscured for a second.

"Another time was when a friend saw me, as she thought, leave my room and house, even rising to go in search of me, but she never fathomed the mystery, and returned to find me sound asleep in bed. I was dressed in a red frock which she recognized. Next day I wrote of the incident to a friend in the U. S. A., whose letter, also written the same day, crossed mine in the mail, arriving two weeks later seemingly solving the mystery—as I had been seen in the United States that same night, the difference in time being allowed for. Remember—I had been seen leaving my house, in England by one friend, and seen arriving in the United States by another, both witnesses unknown to each other mentioning the red dress. The witness in U. S. is, however, now estranged from me because of a well-meant though misunderstood letter, written to him, unknown to me, by a relative.

" . . . I have often awakened just prior to re-entering my physical body after being exteriorized during sleep and am now well acquainted with the preparatory process of the loosening the astral body. Long ago, when I asked if such things could be, I would get such replies as, 'it's only another bat in the belfry!' Then a librarian accidentally gave me your book, The Projection of the Astral Body. Thank you! For I learned from it that if that remark is true, there must be a fair lot of intelligent people 'batty'."

SPENDS SEVERAL DAYS IN SPIRIT WORLD

Most of my readers know of the life work of the Rev. Cora L. V. Richmond, early Peace Conference worker, who, from the age of eleven held large audiences spellbound from lecture platforms throughout the world. On numerous occasions she left her body, once in particular remaining for a prolonged period while her physical form appeared truly cadaverous.

From her account, My Experiences While out of My Body and My Return After Many Days, I make some excerpts, referring those interested to the original for the complete story. After telling of her separation from the physical counterpart she goes on to say:

" . . . Many times, almost numberless, I had experienced the wonderful consciousness of being absent from my human form, of mingling with arisen friends in their higher state of existence. but, until now I had always known that it was only for a brief season and that there was a tie—a vital and psychic tie— binding me to return to my earth form.

" . . . The best beloved, those who had preceded me into this wonderous life, came thronging around to welcome me; not all at once but first those who were by tenderest ties the nearest and the dearest. They did not answer my question: 'Have I really come to stay?' The guide took me gently in charge that I might not even think of the form I had so lately left. A great sense of relief, of being set free from the limitations of the body, filled me.

" . . . My attention was continually attracted to some group that had not been seen by me—always a surprise to find them ALL there. They would smile and seem to answer: 'Yes, all here,' in our own particular states, and doing our own appointed work . . . There was a perception of great light, a consciousness of illumination, an awakening to the vastness of the Realm of Spirit.

"All human sensations, as sight and hearing, are readily perceived by one awakening to spiritual states to be but manifestations of consciousness through the physical limitations to which the spirit in its mental states of earth becomes accustomed. But here all is merged in perception—where one perceives and understands, my guide informed me.

"This added consciousness—uniting or releasing the faculties —is not all at once: I found myself thinking in the accustomed channels, in words as well as thoughts, listening for replies instead of knowing that the answer had been thought to me, really was there before I had questioned . . . I became more and more aware that the whole of me, released from the fetters of the body senses, could perceive and receive more perfectly the answer to every question, even before its formation in thought . . . It is of little avail, however, to attempt to bring into outward forms of thought and expression the perceptions one is aware of while one is in that inner state.

" . . . After a time (I do not know how long) I became aware of being led to where the earthly form was still breathing, being cared for and imbued with breath by a beloved Guardian spirit and by devoted friends in earthly life. I was to return after all! It was necessary to keep my spirit en rapport with the body as the Psychic Cord was not severed that connected body and spirit. But not at once was I to return. These periods of calling my attention to and visiting the body were brief—just enough to keep the vital spark alive, and aid the dear attendants in both worlds to prevent the complete separation which for many days seemed imminent."

Mrs. Richmond states that she met hundreds of persons who

had passed from earth life and that they were working in whatever line of knowledge and work was theirs to attain and achieve
... "It was wonderful to note the ministrations of spirits to those
in other, less fortunate states, especially to those in Earthly
forms. Wherever the ties of consanguinity were also of real
affection the spirit guardians of the household responded to the
'call' perhaps only a thought, a longing, or a silent prayer for
aid and strength, or a need unknown to the one ministered unto.

" ... Spirit states are as varied as are the personal states of
those composing them ... *Time* does not seem to be a factor in
the realm of the spirits except as related to people and events in
the human state with which spirits have connection. It was,
however, a source of continual wonder and surprise to note the
changing forms and atmospheres in the surroundings of those
with whom I was brought in contact.

" ... One whom I had known from early childhood came toward me with a group of his friends and relatives, whom I had
also known. He greeted me as he was ever wont to do when we
both were in Earth forms. Though advanced in years before he
left the form, he was ever youthful, ever calm and peaceful."

This spirit told Mrs. Richmond that "differences of birth,
nationality, outward rank and even of education, are not real
differences in spirit." She also states that she visited the battle-
field, the war being in progress at the time ... " I saw the bright
spots where the ministrants of mercy were rallying, regardless
of nationality or class, to aid those physically wounded, to
breathe a word of comfort to those injured mortally who were
'passing on'. Above the terrible scenes of battle I saw those in
the rank and file ... so suddenly wrenched from their bodies.
Their first thoughts were of those loved ones from whom they
were suddenly parted when ordered to the front."

After witnessing innumerable phases of spirit life, far too
lengthy and involved for me to repeat, Mrs. Richmond noticed
that the visits to her physical counterpart—to recharge it with
the energy of life—were becoming more frequent.

" . . . I prayed to be allowed to remain, to let the body pass: but gradually . . . the garb of the physical body became less repugnant." Eventually she returned to material life again. She continues: ". . . Have you ever visited some fair garden, some sequestered home of dearest friends, a place radiant with beauty and enchantment; where there were flowers massed in rarest combinations of color and fragrance, fountains murmuring in answer to the summer winds, music, such as seemed a part of the enrapturing scene; have you enjoyed this with the chosen friends that alone could make the scene sacred, the best beloved?

"And have you known the reluctance to return to the outer world of daily routine of care, perhaps of pain? Then you know in the smallest degree what it meant to me to return to my bodily form. "

PROJECTS TO SICK FRIEND

On June 19, 1936, Mrs. F. Collins, of Westbury, Wilts, Eng. wrote me saying that she has had experiences out-of-the-body. Several times she has found herself leaving her physical body and travelling to some distant place where she has heard and seen what was taking place there at the time.

The case I here quote was, according to Mrs. Collins, the most striking she ever experienced, for at the time of its happening it was corroborated. She writes:

"I should be pleased for you to publish my experience of astral projection. For want of a better way of expressing it, I seem to be one of those persons whose elements are loosely-knit-together, as I so often have different casual psychic happenings which are entirely unintentional on my part . . . "

Mrs. Collins continues: "One night in bed I was lying in a relaxed and quiescent state preparatory to falling to sleep, when I found myself leaving my physical body and moving or floating toward the house of a friend, who, at that period of my life was a great deal in my thoughts.

100

"I stopped at her house and wandered about outside, and then suddenly found myself in the scullery where I saw my friend walking up and down the room in great pain and very ill. I felt very distressed and tried to help her, but on finding I could not do so, was so frightened that with a violent rush I was back in my body again, shaking violently and suffering from shock. The time was exactly 11:30 p. m.

"The following day, feeling uneasy I called upon my friend and on questioning her she admitted that she had been ill in precisely the manner and at the exact time when I visited her in my astral body."

LIES ON BACK, PROJECTS

In 1930, a friend Miss L—, with whose sane and scientific view-point on all matters pertaining to the occult, I have been impressed, narrated the following to me, although she requests that her name be withheld for fear that her friends and associates might *laugh* should they read it. To say the least we cannot accuse Miss L—, of seeking publicity.

" . . . I am quite convinced that I have had an out-of-the-body experience, although not a very extended one, nor a particularly interesting one; and what surprises me is that since it took place twenty-seven years ago, I have never had a repetition of the same occurrence.

"I was visiting an aunt in Boston at the time and one night I awoke just enough to know where I was. The thought came to me that if I turned over on my back I could get out of my body. So I *did* turn over on my back. Then I fell into the same deep sleep out of which I had been aroused.

"Next I found myself completely conscious and standing on the floor of my room. I should say that my astral self was about eight feet away from my physical self. The room was no brighter than the light afforded by the moon. My next thought was that if I would select some place to go I could go there.

101

"I chose a place (the room of a friend) and found myself there instantly, standing at the foot of the bed. My friend was in the bed and the room was dark, except for the moonlight. I stood there only a short time—then I don't know what became of me. I don't recall if I woke up immediately in my physical body or not. I may have it recorded in my diary which I kept at the time, but being of minor importance it did not stay in my memory . . ."

"There were three periods of consciousness: First, when I awoke and turned over; second, when I found myself projected and standing in my room; third, when I found myself standing in my friend's room . . . I have always been puzzled as to the source of my information or instruction to turn over on my back. It was just a mental impression, a sort of hunch, but I do not see why I had to lie that way . . . At times, while sleeping on my back, I have felt as if I were being held in a vise and would struggle to move . . . "

NOVELIST HAS FIVE PROJECTIONS

A letter dated June 15, 1936 from William Gerhardi the famous novelist with whose works I am sure many of my readers will be familiar, informs me that he has had five out-of-the-body experiences. His novel, "Resurrection" is based upon one of these experiences, and his letter goes on to say: "Though "Resurrection" for reasons stated in the prefatory note, is presented in the form of a novel, the experience is entirely genuine . . . you have my permission to quote me . . . may I take this opportunity of telling you that I have read your book, The Projection of the Astral Body, and find my own experiences tally with yours . . . "

I now quote a portion of Mr. Gerhardi's astral adventure:

" . . . I had been dreaming a dream, so ridiculous, that suddenly it came over me that I must be dreaming . . . 'Now wake' I said, 'and find that there is no need to worry, because it is only a dream'. And I awoke.

102

"But I awoke with a start. For I had stretched out my hand to press the switch of the lamp on the bookshelf over my bed, and instead, found myself grasping the void, and myself suspended precariously in mid-air, on a level with the bookcase. The room, except for the light of the electric stove, was in darkness, but all around me was a milky pellucid light, like steam.

"I was that moment fully awake, and so fully conscious that I could not doubt my senses, astonished as I have never been before, amazed to the point of proud exhilaration. I said to myself, 'fancy that! Whoever would have believed it! And this is not a dream.'

"It seemed almost ludicrous . . . It was as if I were being held up by a steel arm which held me rigid—myself, in comparison, as light as a feather. Next the force which held me up was electrified to a bout of energy by the sudden apprehension which succeeded my first moment of delighted astonishment.

"The swiftness with which I was seized, pushed out horizontally, placed on my feet and thrust forward with the gentle-firm hand of the monitor—'There you are, my good man, now you can proceed on your own'—was something in the highest degree incredible, yet which I cannot doubt . . . Then my body checked its outward movement, turned round. And turning, I became aware for the first time of a strange appendage.

"At the back of me was a coil of light, like a luminous garden hose resembling the strong broad ray of dusty light at the back of a dark cinema projecting on the screen in front. To my utter astonishment, that broad cable of light at the back of me illuminated the very face on the pillows I recognized as my own, as if attached to the brow of the sleeper.

"It was myself, not dead, but breathing peacefully, my mouth slightly open. My cheeks were flushed as if I must have felt hot under those blankets and eiderdown drawn over my shoulder. My hair, lifted by the pressure of the pillow, presented an aspect of my face not familiar to me, never before having seen myself asleep. The face, lying sidewise, and deeply sunk into the pillow, was pathetic and touching in its vacant innocence of expression —and here was I outside it watching it with a thrill of joy and fear. I was awed and not a little frightened to think that I was in the body of my resurrection.

"So that's what it's like? How utterly unforseen! But I was not dead, I consoled myself; my physical body was sleeping peacefully under the blankets while I was apparently on my feet and as good as before. Yet it wasn't my accustomed self, it was as if my mould was walking through a murky, heavy space which, however, gave way easily before my emptiness.

"I had in this mould of mine transgressed into its native fourth dimension, leaving its contents, so to speak, in the third . . . There was this uncanny tape between us, like the umbilical cord, by means of which the body on the bed was kept alive, while its mould wandered about the flat through space which seemed as dense as water. Indeed, in this extraordinarily light body walking seemed like wading through an unsteady sea.

"I staggered uncertainly to the door. I felt the handle, but to my discomfiture I could not turn it; there was no grip in my hand; it seemed unreal. Now, how will I get out? . . . I was pushed forward, the door passed through me, or I through the door, with a marked absence of resistance . . . I caught a glimpse of myself in the mirror as I passed into the bathroom. I looked at my own double and I was dressed exactly as I had gone to bed.

"The only difference was a lack of weight and substance about this body of my continuation. Avidly I went from room to room, trying to collect what proof I could. I was alone in the flat, which was in darkness except for the murky light which seemed to emanate from my own body. . . . I could not hold anything in my hand or displace the lightest of objects and all I could do was to note carefully the position of things—which curtains were open or drawn, the time by the clock in the dining-room, and things of that sort; which all proved correct when I checked them afterward.

". . . Suddenly this strange power . . . began to play pranks on me. I was being pushed up like a half-filled balloon. 'Steady, steady.' I called to myself . . . I was being pushed out with a sort of glee, right out of my flat. Out I flew through the front door and hovered there in the air, a feeling of extraordinary lightness of heart overtaking me. I knew that I could transport myself at will had I now chosen to do so—to New York if I so wished. But a feeling of caution intervened, of fear that something might happen on this long flight and sever my link with the sleeping body to which I wanted to return if only to tell my astounding experience.

" . . . My consciousness became dimmed. It seemed to me as if a dozen coolies, among much screeching and throbbing, were lowering with the utmost precaution under expert direction from a noisy crane, which seemed to reverberate in my own brain, some precious burden which was myself, into some vessel which presently became myself . . . 'Steady, steady', that same monitor who had directed my exploits seemed to be saying, and then with a jerk which shook me as though the machinery dropped into my bowels weighed a ton, I opened my eyes."

Mr. Gerhardi continues: "Since then I have had four other projections. On one of them I actually visited a friend at Hastings and obtained irrefutable proof of having been in his room. On another I visited relations of a friend living at Tunbridge Wells and described them to her accuracy, without my ever having seen them before. On a third, I passed right through a man walking on a lonely road at night. I have not, so far, met a ghost . . . It (projection) has no resemblance to dreaming. If the whole world united in telling me it is a dream I would remain unconvinced . . . "

PROJECTS THROUGH TANK OF MOLTEN GLASS

Aside from his testimony that he has had out-of-the-body experiences, which is our major interest, P. H., a theosophically inclined student of Ohio, gives me some otherwise interesting

105

data. P. H. wants it distinctly understood that there is a difference between projection of the *astral* (desire) body and projection of the *vital* (force) body, maintaining that when projected in the *vital* body one has not yet passed through the atomic web (described by Powell in his *Etheric Double,* page 63).

The vital body equals two-thirds etheric atoms and one-third astral atoms, P. H. claims, while the astral body equals two-thirds astral atoms and one-third etheric atoms.

"I often experience projections of the *vital* body while asleep. I suddenly become conscious at some point quite distant from my home, and have a very vivid clear-cut experience ... An adept told me that one can pass from this state (conscious *vital* projection) onto the astral plane as follows: 'Select some subdivision of the astral, learn all you can about it—scenery, occupants, etc. Visualize it as perfectly as possible. Next ensoul it with all the desire force you can muster. Follow this with a mighty wave of will power, at the same time affirming positively that you enter and become an actor upon this visualized astral plane.'

"When I try this I always lose consciousness and snap back into my physical body again," continues P.H. And in another letter he continues the discussion: "I cannot control my projections and am not conscious of the actual separation, but suddenly awaken at a certain place. *I am then fully conscious, able to turn around and walk about at will.*

"I work in a glass factory and in one experience I went to the factory and while there entered a tank of molten glass. There was no ill effect ... I always snap from projection to full wakefulness in a flash ... I am not aware of the action of the astral cord ... The only time I have fear is when falling. ... A teacher of the Brahmin order to which I belong states that we may know when we achieve true *astral* projection (as opposed to vital projection) because when we have astral projection we will meet our *twin soul* or *guardian* who accompanies us on all astral trips ..."

106

EXPERIMENTS OF OLIVER FOX

From Dr. Carrington's *Introduction* in the book, *The Projection of the Astral Body*, I quote a few portions of his resumé of the experiences of Mr. Oliver Fox who was the only person, aside from myself, ever to give out any detailed, first-hand and scientific directions for voluntary projection of the astral body, at the time.

"Eighteen years ago, when I was a student at a technical college, a dream impelled me to start my research. I dreamed simply that I was standing outside my home. Looking down I discovered that the paving stones had mysteriously changed their position—the long sides were now parallel to the curb instead of perpendicular to it.

"Then the solution flashed upon me: Though that glorious summer morning seemed as real as real could be, I was dreaming. Instantly the vividness of life increased a hundredfold. Never had sea and sky and trees shown with such glamorous beauty; even the commonplace houses seemed alive and mystically beautiful. Never had I felt so absolutely well, so clearbrained, so divinely powerful. The sensation was exquisit beyond words; but lasted only a few moments, and I awoke. As I was to learn later, my mental control had been overwhelmed by my emotions; so the tiresome body asserted its claim and pulled me back. And now I had a wonderful new idea: Was it possible to regain at will the glory of the dream? Could I prolong my dreams?

". . . In practise I found it one of the most difficult things imaginable. A hundred times I would pass the most glaring incongruities, and then at last some inconsistency would tell me that I was dreaming; and always the knowledge brought the change I have described. I found that I could do little tricks at will—levitate, pass through seemingly solid walls, mould matter into new forms, etc.; but in these early experiments I could stay out of my body only for a very short time, and this

107

dream consciousness could be acquired only at intervals of several weeks. To begin with, my progress was very slow; but presently I made two more discoveries:

"1. The mental effect of prolonging the dream produced a pain in the region of the pineal gland—dull at first, but rapidly increasing in intensity—and I knew instinctively that this was a warning to me to resist no longer the call of my body.

"2. In the last moments of prolonging the dream, and while I was subject to the above pain, I experienced a sense of dual consciousness. I could feel myself standing in the dream and see the scenery; but at the same time I could feel myself lying in bed and see my bedroom.* As the call of the body became stronger the dream-scenery became more faint; but by asserting my will to remain dreaming, I could make the bedroom fade and the dream-scenery regain its apparent solidity . . ."

The thought then occurred to Mr. Fox: What would happen if he were to disregard this pain and 'force' his dream-consciousness still further? Not without some trepidation, he finally did so; a sort of *click* occurred in his brain, and he found himself 'locked out' in his dream. He no longer seemed connected with his physical body; the sense of dual consciousness vanished; the ordinary sense of time likewise disappeared, and he found himself free in a new world. *This was his first conscious projection.*

The projection lasted only a short time. Owing partly to the utter sense of loneliness, he experienced a sort of panic and instantly the same strange cerebral *click* was heard and Mr. Fox found himself back in his physical body, completely cataleptic. Gradually he regained control of his organism, moving first one muscle, then another.

Mr. Fox then summed up the possible dangers connected with the experiment and the chief characteristics of his astral

---

*The Dream Body is simply the Astral Body in a semi-conscious condition. Mr. Fox was here having difficulty to bring the projected body truly conscious.—S. M.

projection—how things appeared to him, his emotions, etc. However, up to this time he had never had a projection without a break in consciousness and felt that someone or something was holding him back.

"It was like getting past the 'Dweller on the Threshold.'" Then the solution of the problem suddenly occurred to him: "I had to force my incorporeal self through the doorway of the pineal gland, so that it *clicked* behind me . . . It was done, when in the trance condition, simply by concentrating upon the pineal gland and willing to ascend through it.

"The sensation was as follows: My incorporeal self rushed to a point in the pineal gland and hurled itself against an imaginary trap-door, while the golden light increased in brilliance, so that it seemed the whole room burst into flame. If the impetus was insufficient to take me through, then the sensation became reversed; my incorporeal self subsided and became again coincident with my body, while the astral light died down to normal.

"Often two or three attempts were required before I could generate sufficient will power to carry me through. It felt as though I were rushing to insanity and death—but once the little door had clicked behind me, I enjoyed a mental clarity far surpassing that of earth life. And fear was gone . . . *Leaving the body was then as easy as getting out of bed.*"

(The reader must remember that this was a mental process —an imaginary process if we speak in general terms and Mr. Fox, with admirable scientific caution warns his readers against taking what he says about the pineal gland too literal; but he asserts that these were the exact sensations and he believes that what he asserts is near the truth).

"This then was the climax of my research. I could now pass from ordinary waking life into this new state of consciousness or *from life to death and return without a mental break*. It is easily written but it took fourteen years to accomplish!"

As Carrington states, Mr. Fox mentions three different methods of locomotion in the astral body. The first of these is *Horizontal Gliding* — "accomplished by purely mental effort." Usually this is easy but when the pull of the cord is felt it is anything but effortless;—"it is as though one tugged against a rope of very strong elastic." Mr. Fox also states that whenever he was pulled back into the body, he had the sensation of being drawn *backwards* into it.

The second method of locomotion is a variety of *levitation*, very similar to the typical 'flying dream.' This he describes as "easy and harmless."

The third method he calls "Skrying" and in this he shot upward, like a rocket, with great velocity. It is described as difficult and dangerous. A typical experience of this sort is given in the article.

As to the people encountered on his astral trips, Mr. Fox notes a total absence of "elementals" or other terrifying beings so often said to inhabit the Astral Plane; and the fact that he is nearly always invisible to them ... As to the scenery, this was almost always similar to that seen on the earth, although occasionally unfamiliar scenes were witnessed also.

Mr. Fox maintained that while projected he never could see his physical body — although he could see his wife's very plainly. This fact has been pointed out to me often in the past as evidence against the reality of his exteriorizations. While, as I have pointed out, I am not resorting to explanations in this present volume, there is nothing unusual about this fact whatever. There are many reasons why this could be true which, in fact strengthen, rather than weaken, Mr. Fox's account. In a subsequent volume this will be fully explained.

BELIEVES RHYTHM ASSISTS PROJECTION

I mention briefly some points of possible interest taken from my personal correspondence with a reliable London man, C.B.W., who says:

"Of course I am just as fully convinced of the reality of astral projection as you are, because I have had so many experiences which are as real as my daily life . . . I hope I will be able sometime to talk to you in person as I know you will be able to throw much light on many of the problems I have met with. . . . One thing which puzzles me is that I only become conscious after I am projected to a considerable distance from my body . . ."

C.B.W. gives in detail several seemingly incredible experiences which I have filed away but cannot reproduce at this time, claiming that he once visited a materialization seance and his astral form took on materialization through a Jewish medium; that he saw the ectoplasm, everything and everyone in the room: that on one occasion he visited in Germany and again in India.

C. B. W. is convinced that when "out" he has had the unique experience of seeing and hearing things going on in a specific place through the physical organism of some mortal physically present there! He further believes that his rhythmic dancing, an art at which he spends much time, is somewhat of a motivating influence toward his projections.

"I believe that the transcendental experiences of which I have told you are due in a great measure to my rhythmic inspirational dance movements, solo dances portraying all kinds of music, also, of course, the higher classic. This, I believe sets the etheric or astral or higher mental bodies in a rhythmic vibration with cosmic matter and consequently has something to do with one becoming spiritually conscious in these higher cosmic vehicles . . . "

It will probably be recalled by many readers that Dr. Steiner, in some of his works, mentions the fact that rhythmic music and movements are allied with the awakening of the higher mental factors.

"My experiences are not dreams," C.B.W. states, "or if they are, I am also dreaming right now while I am writing you these lines . . ."

111

A reliable Bristol man L.A.T., who has held a position of considerable responsibility, requiring level-headed management, writes me (Sept. 10, 1936) about a very peculiar and unique experience which occurred to him in 1933 and which he wrote down in his diary at the time. He furnishes me with a copy of the account from his diary, from which I here make a few brief excerpts, for what they may be worth. While the subject says nothing whatever concerning projection, it would appear that in some manner his mind was exteriorized.

L.A.T. had been feeling ill with "flu" and awoke about four o'clock one morning, obsessed with what he calls "an unfounded fear." He reached out, struck a match, and lighted the candle at his bedside, at which time the fear left him. Now feeling at ease he decided to put out the candle again and go to sleep.

". . . But just then I seemed apart from the body on the bed and had no sensation of my heart-beats or feeling of automatic breathing."

While apparently apart from the body on the bed, he states that he seemed to know within himself that he could only keep the body on the bed alive by voluntary breathing, which he found very difficult.

". . . Then stranger still, a third 'I' made its appearance at the foot of my bed! This 'I' at the foot of my bed was fully dressed, except for a hat. I knew it too was 'I,' but a new 'I' . . . This 'I' seemed to be a new resurrection of myself!"

L.A.T. elaborates upon his sensations, emotions, and observations, which I omit, and states that the experience took place while the candle was burning. His experience is very difficult to set forth clearly, but he says: "The real thinking 'I' appeared to be only 'mind' observing what was taking place, from a point to the right of the body on the bed . . ."

PROJECTION OR CLAIRVOYANCE?

Although Mrs. Sidgwick — who never had an out-of-the-body experience, and consequently knew nothing about the various stages of consciousness during projection — has set down the following case as supporting clairvoyance; I am of the opinion that this was a real projection of the astral body in a semi-conscious state. However the reader may judge for himself. The case is unusual: A lady *believes she left her body* and visited her sleeping husband, miles at sea. Curiously enough, at the same time, the husband, dreamed she visited him! And—believe it or not—at the same time a third party saw the phantom lady on the visit!

Mr. S. R. Wilmot sailed from Liverpool to New York, passing through a severe storm. During the eighth night of the storm he had a dream in which he saw his wife come to the door of the stateroom. She looked about and seeing that her husband was not the only occupant of the room, hesitated a little, then advanced to his side, stooped down and kissed him, and after gently caressing him for a few moments, quietly withdrew.

Upon awakening from this dream, Mr. Wilmot was surprised to hear his fellow passenger, Mr. William J. Tait, say to him: "You're a pretty fellow to have a lady come and visit you in this way."

Pressed for an explanation, Mr. Tait related what he had seen while wide awake, lying in his berth. It exactly corresponded with the dream of Mr. Wilmot!

When meeting his wife in Watertown, Conn. Mr. Wilmot was almost immediately asked by her: "Did you receive a visit from me a week ago Tuesday."

Although Mr. Wilmot had been more than a thousand miles at sea on that particular night, his wife asserted: *"It seemed to me that I visited you."* She told her husband that on account of the severity of the weather and the reported loss of another vessel, she had been extremely anxious about him. On the night of the occurrence she had lain awake for a long time and at about four o'clock in the morning it seemed to her that she left her physical self and went out to seek her husband, crossing the stormy sea until she came to his stateroom.

She continued: "A man was in the upper berth, *looking right at me,* and for a moment I was afraid to go in; but soon I went up to the side of your berth, bent down and kissed you, and embraced you, and went away."

A CONSCIOUS PETER IBBETSON

A highly educated and practical professional lady of New York tells me that:

"The moment your most instructive book was published, I bought it, as I was very interested in learning of the experiences of others, aside from myself, in leaving the physical body. I have had the experience several times in my life.

"... The first time, I was conscious the moment I was out of my body. The first thought I had was 'I am dead'... I too found that when I stood too close to my physical I was forcibly drawn back into it. While I was unconscious as I passed in, I was conscious again immediately afterward and was very curious to know how it had happened.

" ... When I was a student in London I used on Sundays to lock myself in my studio and then throw myself on my couch and *leave my body at will,* and could roam about where I pleased ..."

This incident brings to mind the time honored novel *Peter Ibbetson,* by du Maurier. In the story, Peter knows how to dream true. He lies flat on his back with his hands clasped under his neck at the base of the skull, and crossing one leg over the other, goes to sleep — and dreams true. There is a slight analogy here to the dreaming true of projection, discussed elsewhere, and one wonders how much du Maurier really knew about the matter. But, to get back to our correspondent, who goes on to say:

114

"I also used to travel through the air, even out in the country, as does an aeroplane. This travelling was with great speed . . . I could wander (consciously) through the house and watch others although they could not see me . . . Of recent years I have not done this consciously, except now and then while sleeping at night . . ."

AN ENTIRELY CONSCIOUS PROJECTION

For reasons pointed out in the Preface, I quote but one personal experience, and this because it gives a very clear picture of a conscious, from beginning to end, projection. This was in fact my initial projection and while it occurred twenty-one years ago, it was written down at the time and subsequently printed in detail. It was this experience which started me on my investigations in this particular field of psychical research.

I dozed off to sleep one night about ten-thirty o'clock in a perfectly natural manner, and slept several hours. At length I realized that I was slowly awakening, yet could not seem to drift back into slumber nor further arouse. In this bewildering stupor I knew (within myself) that I existed somewhere, in a powerless, silent, dark and feelingless condition.

Still I was conscious — a very unpleasant contemplation of being. I repeat again: I was aware that I existed, but *where* I could not seem to understand. My memory would not tell me. . . I thought I was awakening from natural sleep—but could not seem to proceed. There was but one dominating thought in my mind. Where was I?

Gradually — it seemed an aeon of time, but in reality it was a short interval — I became conscious of the fact that I was lying somewhere. These few half-clear thoughts brought others in their train, and shortly I seemed to know that I was reclining upon a bed, but still bewildered as to my exact location. I tried to move, to determine my whereabouts, only to find I was powerless — as if adhered to that on which I rested.

Eventually the feeling of adhesion relaxed but was replaced by another sensation, equally as unpleasant—that of floating. At the same time my entire body (I thought it was my physical, but it was not) commenced vibrating at a high rate of speed in an up-and-down direction. Simultaneously I could feel a tremendous pulling pressure in the back of my head ... This pressure was very impressive and came in regular spurts, the force of which seemed to pulsate my whole being.

All this was to me like some queer nightmare in total darkness, for, of course, I knew not what was taking place. Amid this pandemonium of bizarre sensations — floating, vibrating, zigzagging and head-pulling, I began to hear somewhat familiar and seemingly far-distant sounds. My sense of hearing was beginning to function. I tried to move, but still could not, as if in the grip of some powerful cryptic directing force.

No sooner had my sense of hearing come into being than that of sight followed. When able to see, I was more than astonished. No words could possibly explain my wonderment. I *was* floating! I was floating in the very air a few feet above the bed. The room, my exact location, was now comprehended. Things seemed hazy at first, but were becoming clearer. I knew well where I was, but could not account for my strange behavior.

Slowly ... I was moving toward the ceiling, all the while lying horizontal and powerless. Naturally I believed that this was my physical body as I had always known it, but that it had mysteriously begun to defy gravity. It was too unnatural for me to understand, yet too real to deny, for being conscious and quite able to see, I had no reason to question my sanity.

Involuntarily, at about six feet above the bed, as if the movement had been conducted by an invisible intelligent force, present in the very air, I was uprighted from the horizontal position, to the perpendicular, and placed standing upon the floor of the room ... where I remained for two or three minutes, still unable to move of my own accord.

Then the unknown controlling force relaxed. I felt free, noticing only the tension in the back of my head. I took a step, when the pressure increased for an interval and threw my body out at an acute angle. I managed to turn around. There were two of me! In the name of common sense — there were two of me! There was another "me" lying quietly upon the bed. It was difficult to conceive of this being real — but there I was, fully conscious, fully able to reason and know what I saw was actual.

The next thing which caught my eye, explained the curious sensation in the back of my head — for my two identical bodies were joined by means of an elastic-like cord, one end of which was fastened to the medulla oblongata region of my phantom counterpart, while the other end centered between the eyes of my physical counterpart. This cord extended across the space of probably six feet which separated us. All this time I was having difficulty to keep my balance, swaying first to one side, then to the other.

Ignorant of the true significance of my condition, my first thought on seeing this spectacle was that I had died during sleep. I made my way, struggling under the magnetic pull of the cord, to where the consanguineous earthly beings lay asleep in another room, hoping to awaken them and let them know of this awful plight. I attempted to open the door, but found myself passing through it. Another miracle to my already astonished mind!

Going from one room to another I tried fervently to arouse the sleeping occupants of the house — but my hands passed through them as if they were but vapors . . . All of my senses seemed normal, save that of touch. I could not make "touchable" contact with things as formerly. An automobile passed the house; I could see it and hear it plainly. After a while the clock struck two, and looking, I saw it registering that hour.

I began to walk about the place still more, filled with the anxiety that morning would come and that then those sleepers would awaken and see me... After about fifteen minutes, I noticed a pronounced increase in the resistance of the cord...

I began to zigzag again under its force, and found, presently, that I was being pulled backward toward my physical body.

Again I found myself powerless to move. Again I was in the grip of the powerful unseen directing power . . . and was resuming the horizontal position, directly over the bed. It was the reverse procedure of that which I had experienced when rising from the bed. Slowly the phantom lowered, vibrating again as it did so. Then it dropped suddenly, coinciding with the physical counterpart once more. At this moment of coincidence, every muscle in the physical organism jerked, and a penetrating pain — as if I had been split open from head to foot — shot through me . . . I was physically alive again, filled with awe, as amazed as fearful, and I had been conscious throughout the entire occurrence . . .

SEES THOUGHT-FORMS WHILE PROJECTED

It is now a fairly well established belief among many that *thought* itself can take on form, which, although not visible to the normal physical eye, is best described as being like a dim mist, evolved from the human mind and exteriorized from the individual. Possibly these thought-forms are what puzzle L. G. T., who does not care to have his name mentioned since he is a dependable professional man of Piccadilly, London. He writes me as follows:

". . . I have been using your book more or less as a text book in my own experiences and experiments which I have conducted over a period of two and one half years . . . I have been working alone . . . and rather in the dark. I do not like to run unnecessary risks, being a family man, and have no one even to talk to who believes or knows anything about this subject . . . "

He continues: "I believe my case is rather unusual. My projections have always been entirely *conscious and voluntary* and never happen after sleep, but always just as I am going to sleep, either during the day or at night . . . I do not seem to be able to

118

get beyond the point I have now reached ... Also I am not often able to check up on what I see while projected because I do not know anyone interested and do not like to broach the subject for obvious reasons ..."

"On several occasions," L. G. T. continues, *"I have noticed that when one is in the astral — thought becomes fact;* that is, what I often *see is really not there, but seems to be a materilization of the thoughts of the person present there at the time.*

"... The getting out process is exactly as you describe it and is always most vivid and comes to me usually within five minutes of lying down. I can have the experiences say every two or three days and have written down the accounts of many of them ..."

AN EXPERIENCE OF CROMWELL VARLEY

It is needless for me to identify Cromwell Fleetwood Varley to my readers in England. But for the information of others I briefly state that he was an English scientist of note, an electrical engineer and the son of Cornelius Varley who was equally as well known.

An inventor of note too, Cromwell Varley invented many ingenious electrical instruments and contributed largely to the success of the second Atlantic cable, after the failure of the first.

Before the Dialectical Society in the year 1869, Varley narrated a veritable case of exteriorization, which occurred to himself. I am indebted to Dr. Nandor Fodor for the account.

Varley was ill, suffering from spasms of the throat, which had been brought on from the fumes of fluoric acid which he used extensively in his scientific work. It was recommended that he have sulphuric ether handy at his bedside to assist breathing in case of a throat spasm.

By smelling of the ether he procured instant relief, but the odour was so unpleasant that he turned to using chloroform. One night he rolled onto his back, the sponge — saturated with chloroform — remaining in his mouth. His wife, Mrs.

Varley, was in a room upstairs, nursing a sick child. Says Varley in his account before the Dialectical Society:

"After a little I became unconscious. *I saw my wife upstairs and I saw myself on my back with the sponge in my mouth,* but was utterly powerless to cause my body to move. I made by my will a distinct impression on her brain that I was in danger. Thus aroused, she came downstairs and immediately removed the sponge and was greatly alarmed.

"I then used my body to speak to her and I said: 'I shall forget all about it and how this came to pass unless you remind me in the morning, but be sure and tell me what made you come down and I shall then be able to recall the circumstance.'

"The following morning she did so, but I could not remember anything about it; I tried hard all day, however, and at length I succeeded in remembering first a part and ultimately the whole experience."

PROJECTED 83 YEARS AGO

It is only through the kind co-operation of my friend James W. Freeman, associate editor of Who's Who in America, in loaning me the book, that I have been enabled to reproduce the out of the body experience of Daniel D. Home, which I quote in abridged form. The volume, long out of print, entitled *Incidents in My Life* was published about seventy-five years ago.

In the summer of 1853 — eighty-three years ago — Home, then a lad of twenty, was in America, residing as a boarder at the Theological Institute at Newbury, on the Hudson. One evening he had gone to bed, pondering on what the world calls *death* when, "an inner perception was quickened within me, till at last, reason was as active as when I was wide awake. I, with vivid distinctness, remember of questioning myself whether I was asleep or not; when, to my amazement, I heard a voice which seemed so natural, that my heart bounded with joy as I recognized it as the voice of one who, while on earth, was far

120

too pure for such a world as ours, and who, in passing to that brighter home, had promised to watch over and protect me . . .

"She said: 'Fear not, Daniel, I am near you; the vision you are about to have is that of death — yet you will not die. *Your spirit must again return to your body in a few hours.* Trust in God . . . all will be well.' Here the voice became lost, and I felt as one who at noonday is struck blind; as he would cling even to the last memories of the sunlight, so I would fain have clung to material existence, not that I felt any dread of passing away, nor that I doubted for a moment the words of my guardian angel, but I feared I had been over-presumptuous in desiring knowledge, the very memory of which might shake my future life.

"This was but momentary, for almost instantly came rushing with a fearful rapidity memories of the past; my thoughts bore the resemblance of realities, and every action appeared as an eternity of existence. During the whole time, I was aware of a benumbing and chilling sensation which stole over my body, but the more inactive my nervous system became, the more active was my mind, till at length I felt as if *I had fallen from the brink of some fearful precipice, and as I fell, all became obscure, and my whole body became one dizzy mass,* only kept alive by a feeling of terror, until sensation and thought simultaneously ceased, and I knew no more.

"How long I lay thus I know not, but soon I felt that I was about to awaken in a most dense obscurity; terror had now given place to pleasurable feeling, accompanied by a certitude of someone dearly loved being near me, yet invisible. It then occurred to me that the light of the spheres must necessarily be more effulgent than our own, and I pondered whether or not the sudden change from darkness to light might not prove painful, for instinctively I realized that beyond the surrounding obscurity lay an ocean of silver-toned light.

"I was at this instant brought to a consciousness of light by

121

seeing the whole of my nervous system,* as it were, composed of thousands of electrical scintillations, which here and there, as in the created nerve, took the form of currents, darting their rayons over the whole body in a manner most marvellous; still, this was but a cold electrical light, and besides, it was external.

"Gradually, however, I saw that the extremities were less luminous, and the finer membranes surrounding the brain became, as it were glowing, and I felt that thought and action were no longer connected with the earthly tenement, but that they were in my spirit body — *in every respect similar to the body which I knew to be mine — which I now saw lying motionless before me on the bed.*

"The only link which held the two forms together *seemed to be a silvery-like light, which proceeded from the brain;* and, as if it were a response to my earlier waking thoughts, the same voice, only that it was now more musical than before, said: 'Death is but a second birth, corresponding in every respect to the natural birth, and should the uniting link now be severed, you could never again enter the body. As I told you, however — this will not be . . . Be very calm for in a few moments you will see us all, but do not touch us; be guided by the one who is appointed to go with you, for I must remain by your body.'

"It now appeared to me that I was waking from a dream of darkness to a sense of light — but such a glorious light! Never did earthly sun shed such rays, strong in beauty, soft in love, warm in life-giving glow. As my last idea of earthly light was the reflex of my own body, so now this heavenly light came from those I saw standing about me. Yet the light was not of their creating, but was shed upon them from a higher source, which only seemed the more adorable . . . to shower every blessing on the creatures of creation. And now I was bathed in light and about me was those for whom I had sorrowed . . . One that I

---

*Davis makes a similar statement in The Magic Staff, p 217

had never known on earth then drew near to me and said: 'You will come with me, Daniel.'

"I could only reply that it was impossible for me to move, inasmuch as I could not feel that my nature had a power over my new spirit body. To this he replied: *'Desire* and you will accomplish your desires which are not sinful—desires being as prayers to the Divinity.'

"For the first time I now looked to see what substantiated my body, and found that it was but a purple tinted cloud! As I desired to go onward with my guide, the cloud appeared as if disturbed by a gentle breeze, and in its movements I was wafted upward until I saw the earth as a vision, far below us.

"Soon I found that we had drawn nearer the earth and were just hovering over a cottage that I had never seen. I saw the inmates but had never met any of them in life. The walls of the cottage were not the least obstruction to my sight—they were only as if constructed of a dense body of air, perfectly transparent . . . I perceived that the inmates were asleep and I saw various spirits watching over the sleepers."

In the original account Home tells other things he witnessed and continues: " . . . I was deeply interested in all this, when my guide said; 'We must now return.' When I found myself near my physical body, I turned to the one who had remained near it and said:

"Why must I return so soon, for it can be but a few moments I have been with you, and I would fain see more and remain here longer?"

" 'It is now many hours,' she replied, 'since you came to us; but here we take no cognizance of time, and as you are here in spirit, you too have lost this knowledge. We would have you with us, but this must not be at present. Return to earth, love your fellow creatures, love truth, and in so doing you will serve God who careth for and loveth all. May the father of mercies bless you Daniel!' "

"I heard no more, but seemed to *sink* as in a swoon, until

123

consciousness was merged into a feeling that earth with all its trials lay before me, and that I . . . must bear my cross . . . And I opened my eyes to material things . . . My limbs were so dead that at least half an hour elapsed before I could reach the bell-rope to bring anyone to my assistance, and it was only by continued friction that, at the end of an hour, I had sufficient force to enable me to stand upright."

Home stated that he had been out of his body eleven hours. "I merely give these facts as they occurred," he concluded, "letting others comment upon them as they may. I have only to add, that nothing could ever convince me that this was an illusion or a delusion . . . "

SOME MISCELLANEOUS CASES

A few miscellaneous items concerning the subject which appeared in the Occult Review shortly after the publication of The Projection of the Astral Body, and elsewhere will fit in nicely here. Of especial interest to this writer is the following testimonial:

"I have read The Projection of the Astral Body, which has cleared up a considerable number of experiences that I have had . . . *I have succeeded in a projection* . . . Having myself now had one, in full possession of all my faculties, which was as real to me as my normal life, anything said to the contrary would make little difference as far as I am concerned . . . "

Signed, J. P. J. Chapman.

This writer has received many many letters similar to the foregoing, most of them going into great detail, but, strange as it may seem, the writers fear having their experiences found out. They fear ridicule from their friends and business associates. So great is their dread of ever having anyone know they were out of their body, since such an occurrence seems unthinkable to the average person, that they will not even allow me to quote their experience. One thing, at least, can be said in favor of this fear, it strongly indicates sincerity on the part of the correspondents, and certainly eliminates the argument that they are trying to get their names before the public.

* * * * *

L. F. of Taranaki, New Zealand writes:* ". . . It is now over 20 years since I first became interested in Spiritism and decided to sit for development. This is the account of what happened: Twice a week at 7:30 I would go alone into the sitting room, get the easiest chair, and just let my body relax, and say to myself, 'now if anyone or anything comes to interfere with you, I will be there instantly.'

"Then resting easy, with eyes closed, one would presently feel them turn up and inward. At this stage one would feel as if the body were non-existent and the mind quicker in every way. One would feel no chair nor anything else; yet if anyone came into the room one would be aware if they spoke. I might have answered with an effort, but it was apt to break conditions.

"Still keeping that state a little longer, it suddenly seemed as if the whole house would disappear and I found myself outside. Then I would say: 'I'll just have a look around,' and (in my subtle body) make for a gate on the other side of the little field . . . After crossing the field, there was no need for me to open the gate. How I knew this, I do not know. I would pass right through! After about three chains more I would find myself saying: 'Now Louie, you have just begun these sittings—better not go too far just yet.'

After that I would find myself back in my physical body and much awake. That happened a good many times—just the

---

*Occult Review.

125

same spot reached. Yet I knew I could *will* myself to go on if I had dared. It must have been fear that kept me back . . . I dropped the practise for three months, then could not do it again."

* * * * *

An excerpt from an article *Native Psychism in South Africa* by I. Toye Warner-Staples, F. R. S. A. reads:*

" . . . Another curious case of deep trance occurred to a Basuto evangelist, the Rev. Walter Matiti, who told his congregation on the Reef that fourteen years previous he had been very ill and died. At least, so thought his friends at the time, as his heart had ceased to beat. He saw his (physical) body stretched out on a mat, and a group of men and women weeping around it.

"All of the events of his life were presented to him and his spirit guide told him to repair the evils he had done. He saw various countries and the coast of Africa as he passed over them with his guide. He was told to preach to every tribe, irrespective of creed, and after the trance ended and he returned to (physical) consciousness he could speak many languages! "

* * * * *

Here is an absorbing though brief case where the astral and mental bodies (Theosophically speaking) were exteriorized according to the subject.*

"Some time back," writes A. R. D., "I found myself outside of my body, looking at it. I then wished to know how one got out and in, etc. Then one night I again found myself out, and saw my astral come out, gather itself together, hover over the physical, and float out of the room through the closed window.

"I—my mental self, I suppose—then joined it and seemed

---

*Ibid

to feel a friend was waiting for me. We rose high and soared all about the town. We then entered a door, and went through the rooms. I said, 'Why this is my house,' and laughed until I was awake. A friend had told me that getting out of and into the body was painful. This I could not believe. I fancy the experience was to satisfy myself. I have not done it again consciously . . . "

* * * * *

This curious case, reported by Myers in *Human Personality* appears to indicate that the mentality, the actual consciousness does at times slip out of its physical abode unknown to the subject. I reproduce the written statement of the subject in question, Mrs. Stone, who says:

"When about nine or ten years old I was sent to school in Dorchester as a day border. It was there I had my first curious experience that I clearly remember. I was in an upper room in the school standing with some others in a class opposite our teacher Miss Mary Lock.

"Suddenly I found myself by her side, and, looking toward the class saw my (physical) self distinctly—a slim, pale girl, in a white frock and pinafore. I felt a strong anxiety to get back, as it were, but it seemed a violent and painful effort, almost struggle when accomplished."

It will be recalled that Mr. Wills in his account mentioned of looking over the dentist's shoulder into his own mouth. A strikingly similiar testimony.

* * * * *

J. Arthur Hill, in *Man is Spirit*, tells of a Miss Hinton who, at the age of seventeen, was put under chloroform in order that some of her teeth might be removed. Her return to consciousness was delayed, resulting in much alarm, but when she did awaken she said that she had been *above* her physical body, around which those present were gathered, and that she had tried without success, to talk to them. Supposing herself dead she wondered why she was not being judged!

* * * * *

Again there was the case of Dr. George Wyld. He had been inhaling chloroform to allay the pain of passing a small renal calculus, when he was astonished to find himself clothed, possessed of normal reasoning faculties, and standing about two yards away observing his own motionless physical form upon the bed.

He was enabled to understand the significance of the revelation while standing there and later learned that others were able to corroborate his experience, which brought him to the conclusion that sensation is centered in the subtle body and that the effect of an anæsthetic is to drive that body out of its physical shell, thus rendering the latter incapable of feeling pain.

* * * * *

In *Light*, Miss Gibbs tells a unique story which originally came from Miss Dallas who can vouch for the accuracy of it. While it is true that other explanations besides that of projection of the astral body, can be put forth, certainly none are more appropriate. However, we will not argue the matter, I offer the incident merely as evidence. Simply stated it is this:

A certain man, whom we will call A—, had been visiting at a country parsonage. After he left the place, other guests arrived. They held a circle with the *table*. The table announced that it was being moved by A—, the man who had formerly been visiting the place. He (A—'s, projected astral self which was supposed to be moving the table) was asked many questions, and he replied, giving the sitters the knowledge that he had been

128

out shooting in the afternoon and had been playing billiards with his father in the evening! He stated that 'his soul' was with them at the parsonage, but his body was at home!

On communicating with A—, physically, later, the incident was confirmed, and he added: "After playing billiards I lay down on the couch, in the billiard and dreamed that I was back in the parsonage.*

* * * * *

The Rev. W. Maitland (ibid) tells of the experiences of two clergymen in his neighborhood:

"Firstly, a rector in Norfolk, a man possessed of very considerable psychic power. He has often manifested the power of astral projection. He once spent some time in a Retreat in London, during which time he was cut off from all contact with the outside world, even to the extent of seeing no newspapers.

"On his last night in the Retreat, *this man became aware that he had left his material body.* He found himself in what he knew must be a large Northern town. He made his way to what he knew was the goal, entered it and went straight to the condemned cell, where he felt his spiritual work was to bring help to the soul of the man who was to be executed early next morning.

"The following day, the Rector, on leaving the Retreat, bought a newspaper and was at once confronted with the account of the criminal's execution at 8 a. m. that morning in Newcastle Goal."

"Second, we have a country rector who has been in close communication with the spirit-world for many years . . . He belongs to no Spiritualistic Society, and takes no Spiritualistic papers—it has just been forced upon him through the mediumship of himself and his family. *He told me he had the experience*

---

*In this connection see, *The Projection of the Astral Body;* also my article, *The Crypto-Conscious Mind and Telekinesis,* (Occult Review March-April 1930) *of leaving his body,* especially when suffering acute pain, as he often does, and that his wife has similar powers . . . "

* * * * *

Do animals have a subtle body which can be exteriorized? A rather curious case which might be considered to come within the bounds of testimony for projection was reported by M. D. of Sydney, Australia, in *The Harbinger of Light.* Briefly, M. D.'s story is that on going to England she paid a visit to the well known psychic photographer, Mr. Hope, of Crewe, and sat for a photograph.

"The result of the sitting was a photo of myself with two *extras* surrounded by a cloudy mist in the background. The one—a recently passed over relative (in New South Wales) and easily recognized;—the other a small dog's face, partly showing. Besides these two *extras* there is a perfect shadow form of a silky terrier poised on my shoulder—quite different in effect to the solid looking forms of the *extras.*"

M. D. states that on going to London she obtained a sitting with a well known medium, where a deceased relative who had appeared on the picture communicated with her. He gave his name, and told her how glad he had been that he was enabled to show himself. Regarding the two dogs which appeared on the photo, the communicator stated that one of them was *Lassie* who had predeceased him.

As to the other one, it was *Bully*—a dog still living in the flesh. *The communicator asked M. D. to tell his widow Flo that he had stolen Bully while the latter was asleep.* In other words we are told that while this earthly dog, Bully, was sleeping, a disembodied spirit took out the astral body of this dog and it appeared with him on the spirit picture.

"The remarkable part of the picture is the difference in form between Lassie and Bully," M. D. continues. The former, having

130

died is solid looking, and the latter (still alive) is shadowlike. Bully's foot was twisted in an accident some years ago. The defect shows in the photograph!"

While attending a seance in South Africa, Dr. Hegy, author of *A Witness Through the Ages,* inquired if it would be possible for him to communicate, through the Medium, with the spirit of someone still living on earth. He was informed that it could be done, and at the next seance, sure enough—two ghosts of the living were announced. The first stated that he was a convict serving time in England.

The second communicator told Dr. Hegy that he lived in London and was a bricklayer, though unemployed. He gave his full name and address and told the Doctor that he was and had been in ill health. He informed him that he had broken a leg and as a result walked with a limp; that he was also blind in one eye. He even asked Dr. Hegy his opinion on the case and inquired concerning the treatment he had received at the hospital.

Dr. Hegy wrote to the London address given him by the apparent ghost of a living man, but received no reply. Time passed. Two years ago, Dr. Hegy, while in London, went to the address where he found the man, whose spirit was supposed to have communicated with him, and discovered that he not only walked with a limp but that every other detail given at the seance in South Africa—three pages in all—was absolutely correct. The letter had also been received by the man, but the latter had been too awed to answer it!

*   *   *   *   *

In March 1930, a lady living in Boston wrote a letter to Dr. Carrington which was passed on to me by the latter. While containing nothing startling, and merely *another person vouching for the reality of astral projection,* I quote a fragment from her message which sets forth how her experiences came about:

"I wanted to stop after your Ford Hall lecture last Sunday

and tell you how much I enjoyed it, but there were too many ahead of me . . . I was particularly interested in what you told us about the young man who had experiences in projecting the astral body.

"It is the first time I ever heard my own experiences duplicated—though he went further than I . . . I happened upon this (projection) by chance, I suppose, as a result of sleepless nights. I found that by drawing the sense of vision back into the brain and looking at the inside of my face, I could drop off to sleep and watch myself reach the extreme edge. A few years of this and I occasionally *went over* consciously.

" . . . I could never do anything with the Peter Ibbetson method . . . But I did hear the President of the Theosophical Society say, in a lecture he gave some years ago here in Boston that the proper position to take was on one's back, chin in, ankles crossed and hands also, hands over the solar plexus, right over the left if left handed and vise versa. My own position was entirely different and perhaps less successful for that reason. I always found more heart discomfort on my back . . . "

* * * * *

Speaking as I did in the preceding account of *merely another person vouching for the reality of astral projection*, I am reminded that Vout Peters often told a story of how a mortal friend of his was able to materialize through a medium and appear to him; and no less a personage than William T. Stead has related a similiar incident; while the great Emanuel Swedenborg claimed to have made many many trips out of his body. D. D. Home appeared to Count and Countess Tolstoy at a railway station, three hours before his actual arrival.

* * * * *

Then again, Professor Schiller in a report published in the S. P. R. *Journal*—which he too vouches for—tells of a lady in a *home* suffering from mental derangement and extreme old age, who is able to communicate with relatives very sanely through a medium, while at the same time she seemed to realize she would be mentally unsound on returning to the physical body!

* * * * *

A missionary in Africa narrated the following which is quoted by Dr. Paul Joire in *Psychical and Supernormal Phenomena*:
"A Ugema Uzago chief of the tribe Jabikou, threw himself into a state of catalepsy, after a magical ceremony, before the missionary, so he would be enabled to attend a meeting of the disciples of the Master on the Yemvi plateau—a distance of four days' walk.
"The missionary asked him to deliver a message on his way, to a black merchant in the village of Ushong—a distance of three days by foot. On awakening from his cataleptic state Ugema Uzago declared that he had delivered the message. Three days later the black merchant appeared and declared that Ugema knocked at his door in the night and as he did not open, shouted in the message of the missionary!"

* * * * *

The ever popular editor, Ernest W. Oaten, in a letter to me dated September 7, 1936, makes the casual comment that, "I am keenly interested in (projection) as I have had many such experiences myself. I have frequently projected the double, and discovered incidents which were going on many miles from me. I have further appeared to my wife and my brother, not by pre-arrangement, but quite spontaneously and by my own definite act of will . . . "

* * * * *

Eugene Osty tells of a case narrated by M. Charles Quarter in which he saw his own body, apparently lifeless, hanging in a dangerous position on the sofa. He, in spirit, tried to lift up his physical self but was quite unable to do so; so he decided to go and ask his mother to help. The mother was at the time involved in a conversation and stopped short saying: "I believe my son is calling me!" Needless to say, the son interiorized again.

* * * * *

Mr. Brackett, the author of *Materialized Apparitions* tells us that he has seen hundreds of materialized forms and "in many cases I have seen the ethereal body of the medium also, so like him that I would have sworn that it *was* the medium, had I not seen his double dematerialize in my presence and afterward assured myself that he was asleep . . . "

The present author pointed out in his former work that the form seen in materialization seances is often, without doubt, the exteriorized astral body of the medium. At that time I also wrote:

"I am acquainted with an old occultist, Carl Pfuhl, who told me that, on one occasion, a little girl who was sleeping in a hammock, outside the seance room . . . materialized and claimed to be the daughter of a member of the circle—who had a daughter about the same age who had passed away. Yet the form seen was that of the girl sleeping in the hammock outside, and had not been in any way transformed to represent the girl she claimed to be. The girl who slept in the hammock knew nothing of it, on awakening . . . We know that thought can affect the form of the astral body, and it might be just possible that some spirit wishing to manifest could possibly impress the unconscious form of the astral body into its own likeness." This is, however, purely speculative, and not offered as evidence for projection, but merely as an interesting suggestion.

Incidentally, Sir William Crookes, made a similar observation, and in writing of experiments with Mrs. Fay, the medium, said:

" . . . The curtain was withdrawn sufficient for me to see the person who held it (his book) out to me. It was the form of **Mrs. Fay** completely (whom Crookes had under electric test control) and at this moment the galvanic current did not register the slightest interruption . . . "

FAMOUS AUTHOR VISITS ETERNITY

One of the most astonishing out-of-the-body adventures was that of William Dudley Pelley, the famous American author. Mr. Pelley's story of his projection first appeared in the American Magazine of March 1929, where, it is estimated almost ten million people read it, before it later was reproduced in a handsome little brocture entitled, "Seven Minutes in Eternity —With Their Aftermath." *

Almost immediately letters by the thousands were received by Mr. Pelley, from all sections of America and England and from all classes of persons. Hundreds claimed to have had similar experiences. Over 144 sermons were known to have been made by clergymen concerning the experience; and a fact which particularly astonished Mr. Pelley was that out of all the resulting mail, less than 24 of the communications derided him.

I cannot more than touch upon the experience here and I most heartily urge all of my readers to read the entire fascinating account. Prior to the occurrence, Mr. Pelley was a case-hardened Materialist. He retired one evening in April 1928, at his bungalow in the Sierra Madre Mountains near Pasadena, California, feeling quite normal in every respect.

"But between three and four in the morning, a ghastly inner shriek seemed to tear through my somnolent consciousness. In despairing horror I wailed to myself: 'I'm dying! I'm dying!' What told me, I don't know. Some uncanny instinct had been unleashed in slumber to awaken and apprise me . . . a physical

---

*Collier

135

sensation which I can best describe as a combination of heart attack and apoplexy.

"Mind you, I say physical sensation. This was *not* a dream. I knew that something had happened either to my heart or head—or both—and that my conscious entity was at the mercy of forces over which I had no control . . . "

The author tells how he plunged down a mystic depth of blue space in his phantom body, while queer noises sang in his ears, and he said to himself: "So this is death . . . My dead body may lie in this lonely house for days before anyone discovers it."

Next he found himself whirling madly and had the same sensation which he had once experienced when in an airplane which went into a tailspin; but at this juncture two persons—in spirit —came to his assistance, one of them saying: "Take it easy old man. Don't be alarmed. You're all right. We're here to help you."

The two spirit friends carried him in their arms and laid him on a beautiful marble-slab pallet where they stood over his nude (astral) body until he had regained his strength. They smiled knowingly at his confusion and chagrin, and exchanged good-humored glances as they told him not to try to see everything in the first seven minutes.

Of especial interest is the way in which his astral body became clothed. His friends told him to bathe in a pool near the portico. He did so . . . "And here is one of the strangest incidents of the whole adventure . . . When I came up from the bath I was no longer conscious that I was nude. On the other hand, neither was I conscious of having donned clothes. The bath did something to me in the way of clothing me. What, I don't know."

Says Mr. Pelley: " . . . I found myself an existing entity in a locality where persons I had always called *dead* were not dead at all. They were very much alive . . . "

He tells at great length of the wonderful things which he witnessed in the realm of the so-called dead, where he was "conscious of a beauty and loveliness of environment that surpasses chronicling on paper."

" . . . Think of all the saintly, attractive, magnetic folk you know, imagine them constituting the whole social world . . . and the whole of life permeating with an ecstatic harmony as universal as air, and you get an idea of my reflections in those moments."

He continues: " . . . I pledge my prestige and reputation that I talked with these people, identified many of them, called others by their wrong names and was corrected, saw and did things that night . . . that it is verboten for me to narrate in a magazine article . . . "

In another place he says: "There is a survival of the human entity after death of the body for I have seen and talked intelligently with friends whom I have looked down upon as cold wax in caskets."

He resented having to return to his earthly body, but finally his astral visit terminated.

" . . . I was caught in a swirl of bluish vapor that seemed to roll in from nowhere in particular. Instead of plunging prone I was lifted and levitated. Up, up, up I seemed to tumble, feet first . . . A long, swift, swirling journey of this. And then something clicked. Something in my body. The best analogy is the sound my repeating deer-rifle makes when I work the ejector mechanism—a flat, metallic, automatic sensation . . . "

"I was sitting up in my physical body."

That all this was a real conscious experience and not a dream, Mr. Pelley well knew and on this point he states: "I am not given to particularly graphic dreams. Certainly we never dream by the process of coming awake first . . . "

Then came the aftermath. William Dudley Pelley, as all who know him testify, has since been a changed man in every respect —physically, mentally, and spiritually. While remarkable physical changes took place within him, more remarkable still were the latent psychic powers which were unlocked to enable him to "tune in" with minds on other dimensions.

137

"I can," he says, "proffer questions and get sensible and oftimes invaluable answers."

He has, for example, "tuned in" and written down 10,000 word lectures on abstruse aspects of science, cosmology and metallurgy; has taken down a message in which an erudite philologist found over a thousand words of pure Sanscrit, etc.

"I should already be the wisest man on earth," he states, "if I could be credited with fabricating this material from my own subconscious mind."

LEARNS TO PROJECT VOLUNTARILY

In his first letter to me, dated August, 11, 1929, Mr. Arthur J. Wills, an architect and C. E. of Chicago, Illinois, writes:

" . . . All of my experiences were involuntary, though I tried voluntary projection in ignorance of how to go about it . . . On one occasion at a dentist's office, without anæsthetic, as he drilled into my tooth, the pain became so acute that I actually 'lost myself'. Suddenly I found myself looking over the dentist's shoulder into my own mouth!

"Four years ago I was with a firm which had a temporary office in an old building. One night I fell asleep, to find myself later projected into the old building—going through it, up the stairs, etc. I was as fully conscious as I ever was in my life. The light was greyish. As I wandered about I noticed that no one was at work. The thought struck me, 'it is the middle of the night. What am I doing here?' And with that thought I was transferred back to my physical body.

" . . . Three years ago, while travelling on a train from Davenport to Minneapolis, I lay down on the seat and went to sleep. Presently I found that I was propping myself up—physically, I thought, until I discovered otherwise. I could see the passengers behind me as easily as those in front of me; some slept, some read, etc.

"Then I saw that it was not my physical body in which I was

138

consciously propped up (by my right arm) ; for, looking downward, I saw my body still sleeping on the seat! For a few moments I enjoyed and admired this new and beautiful body (the astral), which was rosy pink, glowing like a luminous pearl. Something which looked like an 'arm' seemed to run down and merge into the brain of the physical body. In a short time I was back in my physical body again. Sitting up and looking around, I saw the passengers back of me, just as I had seen them from my luminous body . . . There seemed to be no procedure by which I could learn to project at will . . . "

After the foregoing was written, Mr. Wills, who studied the modus operandi for the production of the phenomenon as published by this author, writes, on December 15, 1929:

"I have experienced it (projection) voluntarily of late. I awake in the astral body, fully conscious, but after the body has projected, and I do not experience the intermediate stages of which you speak . . . If I think emotionally of my physical self while *out* I am instantly back into it again as a rule . . . Have done things while projected which would be physically impossible, such as defying gravity, and being suspended in mid-air . . . Once I walked down a corridor where scene after scene of history passed in front of my eyes . . . When, while projected at a great height, I realize there is no physical support under me, I sometimes have a feeling of nausea.

" . . . If this realization (of non-support) comes slowly, so that I can reason that the sensation is merely an attribute of the physical body apart from the 'me', the real entity, I can overcome it and retain passivity. But if the realization comes suddenly, I return to the physical speedily with a shock, causing a jerk of the body . . . As yet I cannot control circumstances while out. I never know where, who, or what I may contact or observe. I find myself merely a detached, rational intelligence, observing, noting, and comparing what is actually about me.

" . . . On October 29 I went to bed, tried to project, and did so. My astral body went out diagonally, toward the right, and

139

presently I found myself amid multi-colored rocks and trees which were dripping wet with rain. I thought about my physical body lying in bed, while here I was *out* in another body at the same time.

"I tried to assure myself that everything would be all right, as you pointed out in your book, but nevertheless I had a slight feeling of alarm. My astral body was white, as if draped. I lifted my hand and said: 'My trust is in God,' and on doing so the fear passed away . . . I began to move at a fair speed, passed the rocks and trees, finally arriving on a paved wet street.

"As I passed along I drew aside as if I were afraid the wet branches, if touched, would cause drops of rain to fall upon me. I left the street and crossed the lawn. Just then I saw a glowing sky-blue colored cloud on the lawn. A wish came to me that I could see my wife, who had passed away some months before, and I seemed to know instinctively that she was in that cloud. As I approached nearer to it I began to lose consciousness and was returned to my physical body . . . It was really raining outside . . . "

Mr. Wills tells of consciously projecting to his sister's home in England, while, "at the same time I knew that my physical body was in bed in U. S. A., and to prevent my instinctive return before I was ready to go, I kept saying to myself: 'Steady now, it's all right. Let us see what we can find out.' I walked out of the bathroom, into the bedroom where I used to sleep and wandered about . . . I walked along the corridor a short distance where I was stopped. Flesh-like arms were barring me from going further.

"I could not distinguish who it was, but tried to push those arms out of the way. My own arms seemed to merge into and become a part of those which were barring me, though at right angles. I was greatly irritated at this and pushed and protested vigorously . . . In the struggle I became unconscious."

Mr. Wills further says: " . . . In dreams there is always a sense of confusion and disorder, as if one had nothing fixed or concrete to tie to, and on awakening there is the immediate realization of having been deluded by the somnolent mind. In projection I find none of this. At first the sensation of being in different conditions tends to arouse the emotions, which usually return one to the physical.

"But when the emotions are controlled or dismissed from the consciousness one is quite normal and rational. Consciousness is not only self-evident but enlarged, reasoning faculties are rendered more acute, there is no delusion about it . . . One is never more clear-minded and intelligent than when projected and conscious . . . Yet all this sounds as 'crazy' as Columbus' idea of travelling straight West on a flat world, when the scientists 'knew' he would fall over the edge . . . "

VISITS RELATIVES IN SPIRIT WORLD

In 1931 I received a letter from Mr. Maurice A. Craven, head of Maurice A. Craven and Company of Pawtucket, R. I. in which he gave me his permission to relate here an experience which he underwent a few years before.

In his account, Mr. Craven states that he felt very depressed one day and the following night, shortly after going to sleep, he became conscious of the fact that a strange 'someone' had taken a powerful hold on his arm.

"Don't be afraid—don't be afraid," the entity kept repeating in monotone, according to Mr. Craven, who continues:

"I felt myself going upward as if I were in an express elevator. Finally I stopped, but was not permitted to look behind me. My invisible guide walked with me down the most beautiful boulevard I ever saw. On either side there were magnificent trees and the homes were gorgeous and like white marble.

"My guide took me through a lovely garden to where there was an oddly shaped summer-home. To my surprise my grandfather and grandmother both came out and welcomed me. We

141

had a long conversation about many things which we all remembered."

Mr. Craven tells how his grandparents told him that before he went they wanted him to visit Lily, Vinnie and Charlie—his aunts and uncle who had long ago passed away.

" We continued walking down the street of magnificent trees and houses, passing many persons and crowds of persons. They all seemed very happy and smiled either at me or my guide. Finally we arrived at the homes of my other relatives and they too were glad to see me.

"As we went along I saw a place where a beautiful home was in the process of construction. Who was building it, how it was being built, what material was being used, I am at a loss to know; but grandfather told me it was being prepared for our family.

"I distinctly remember of asking them how they lived—what they ate—but they only smiled knowingly at me and replied that the air was vitalized for them, that they needed nothing, and that their work was a labor of love.

"I did not go back to my body the way I came. I entered a large coach where I found a handsome lounge inside. I was told to lie down there for a while and in coma I was transported back to my bed . . . The memory of my journey will live with me until I am ready to go over into the Great Beyond."

PART THREE

THE VERITY CASE

In this case the initials only are used, but the writer of the account was known to the officers of the S. P. R. who guarantee his trustworthiness. The incident has been so oft-quoted that I would not repeat it here again save for the fact that I wish to refer back to it in discussing the objections of Professor Charles Richet. On the other hand, it is interestingly unique in that the projected double was produced experimentally (intentionally) and was seen collectively (by two percepients).

"On a certain Sunday evening, in November 1881, I, having been reading of the great power of which the human will is capable of exercising, determined with the whole force of my being that I would present in spirit in the front bedroom of the second floor of a house situated at 22 Hogarth Road, Kingston, in which room slept two young ladies of my acquaintance, namely, Miss L. S. V., and Miss E. C. V., aged respectively twenty-five and eleven years.

"I was living at the time at 23 Kildare Gardens, a distance of about three miles from Horagth Road, and I had not mentioned in any way my intention of trying this experiment to either of the ladies, for the simple reason that it was only on retiring to rest upon this Sunday night that I made up my mind to do so. The time at which I determined to be there was one o'clock in the morning and I had a strong intention of making my presence perceptible.

"On the following Tuesday I went to see the ladies in question, and in the course of my conversation, without any allusion to the subject on my part, the elder one told me that on the previous Sunday night she had been much terrified by perceiving me standing by her bedside, and that she screamed out when the apparition advanced toward her, and awoke her little sister

145

who also saw me. I asked her if she was awake at the time and she replied most decidedly in the affirmative, and, upon my inquiring the time of the occurrence, she replied, 'at about one o'clock in the morning.'

"This lady, at my request, wrote down a statement of the event, and signed it." Mr. Gurney (one of the authors of *Phantasms of the Living*) became deeply interested in these experiments, and requested Mr. S. H. B. to notify him in advance on the next occasion when he proposed to make his presence known in this strange manner. Accordingly, March 22, 1884, he received the following letter:

Dear Mr. Gurney:

I am going to try the experiment tonight of making my presence perceptible at 44 Morland Square, at 12 p. m. I will let you know the result in a few days.

Yours very sincerely,
S. H. B.

The next letter, which was written April 3, contained the following statement, prepared by the recepient, Miss L. S. Verity:

"On Saturday night, March 22, 1884, at about midnight, I had a distinct impression that S. H. B. was present in my room, and I distinctly saw him, being quite awake. He came toward me and stroked my hair. I voluntarily gave him this information when he called to see me on Wednesday, April 2, telling him the time and circumstances of the apparition without any suggestion on his part. The appearance in my room was most vivid and quite unmistakable."

Miss A. S. Verity also furnishes this corroborative statement: "I remember my sister telling me that she had seen S. H. B., and that he touched her hair, before he came to see us on April 2."

The agent's statement of the affair is as follows: "On Saturday, March 22, I determined to make my presence perceptible

146

to Miss V. at 44 Morland Square, Notting Hill, at 12 midnight; and, as I had previously arranged with Mr. Gurney that I should post him a letter on the evening on which I tried my next experiment (stating the time and other particulars) I sent him a note to acquaint him with the above facts. About ten days afterward I called upon Miss Verity, and she voluntarily told me that on March 22, at twelve o'clock, midnight, she had seen me so vividly in her room (whilst wide awake) and that her nerves had been much shaken, and she had been obliged to send for a doctor in the morning."

WHERE WAS LURANCY'S SPIRIT?

He who has not read of the Watseka Wonder has missed one of the most convincing documents ever compiled in favor of spiritism and the possibility of a spirit of the dead taking possession of the body of a mortal. Presupposing such a possibility the question which seems to have been overlooked is: Where is the spirit of the mortal during this time of possession? Does it remain in the body or is it dislodged from the body?

The main facts in the case of Lurancy Vennum (The Watseka Wonder) follow: Lurancy Vennum, a young girl living with her parents at Watseka, Illinois began having a series of spasms accompanied by a purely physical ailment. Her condition grew worse and finally she developed clairvoyant vision and was apparently obsessed by lowly quarrelsome personalities.

Popular opinion in Watseka was that Lurancy was insane, in fact a Methodist minister, Rev. B. M. Baker wrote an insane asylum to make arrangements for taking her in. It happened, however, just at this juncture, that a townsman, Mr. Asa D. Roff (believing the case to be one of spirit possession) persuaded Mr. Vennum to allow Dr. E. Winchester Stevens, of Janesville, Wisconsin to investigate the case of his daughter, to which Mr. Vennum consented.

Dr. Stevens went to Watseka and with Mr. Roff observed

Lurancy during her states of possession, talked directly with the entities obsessing her—who claimed to be spirits of the dead—and was himself convinced that they actually were. From, *The Watseka Wonder** where I take all of my quotations, I abbreviate:

" . . . About half-past five, p. m. the visitors arose to depart; she (Lurancy) also arose flung up her hands and fell to the floor. . . . He (Dr. Stevens) by magnetic action, soon had her under perfect control," and was soon, "in full and free communication with the sane mind of Lurancy Vennum herself . . . She answered the Doctor's questions with reference to herself, her seemingly insane condition, and the influences which controlled her . . . She regretted having such evil controls around her. She said she knew the evil spirit calling itself Katrina and Willie and others."

Dr. Stevens told her that it might be possible to induce some more intelligent and upright spirit to control her, and on being advised, she looked about—inquired of those she saw—described and named them—hoping to find some entity present who would be willing to come and keep the evil ones from annoying her. Then she said to the mortals present: "There are a great many spirits near who will gladly come," and she proceeded to give the names and description of persons long since deceased, some she had never known but who were known by those older persons present. She said there was one in particular who wanted to come and had been designated by "higher -ups" to come whose name was Mary Roff.

Mr. Roff being present said: "That is my daughter! Mary Roff is my girl—why, she has been in heaven twelve years! Yes, let her come, we'll be glad to have her come."

The next morning Mr. Vennum called at the office of Mr. Roff, greatly excited, and told him that the girl (the consciousness in Lurancy's physical body) claimed to be Mary Roff. That she

---

*Austin Publishing Company, Los Angeles, California.

wanted to go home. That she "seemes like a child real homesick, wanting to see her 'pa' and 'ma' and brothers."

We read: "From the wild angry ungovernable girl to be kept only by lock and key . . . the girl has now become mild, docile, polite and timid, knowing none of the family, but constantly pleading to go home. The best wisdom of the family was used to convince her that she was at home and must remain—but she would not be passified."

" . . . About a week after she took control of the body, Mrs. Asa B. Roff and her married daughter Mrs. Minerva Alter, hearing of the remarkable change, went to see the girl. As they came in sight, far down the street, the girl, looking out the window, exclaimed exultingly, 'Here comes ma and sister Nervie!' the name she had called Mrs. Alter in girlhood. As they came into the house, she caught them around the necks, wept and cried for joy and seemed so happy to meet them . . . From this time on she was only more homesick than ever."

Eventually the situation became so unbearable for all concerned that it became necessary to allow the girl (claiming to be Mary Roff, in the body of Lurancy Vennum) to go and live with the Roffs.

"On the eleventh day of February, they sent the girl to Roffs where she convinced them that she was their natural daughter. On being asked how long she would stay she said: 'The angels will let me stay till sometime in May.' And she made it her home there for three months and ten days, a happy contented daughter and sister in a borrowed body . . . knowing every person and everything that Mary knew when in her original body twelve years to twenty-five years ago, recognizing and calling by name those who were friends and neighbors of the family from 1852 to 1865 . . . calling their attention to scores, yes hundreds of incidents that transpired during her natural life. During all of her sojourn at Mr. Roff's she did not recognize any of the Vennum family."

Again we read: "So natural did it seem to her that she could

149

hardly believe that this was not her own original body born nearly thirty years ago."

As to the numerous incidents and proofs which established the identity of the original Mary Roff, I cannot here concern myself. They are fully set forth in the cited volume by Dr. E. Winchester Stevens, Mr. Roff and others.

On the seventh of May, the possessor of the body (Mary Roff) told her mother (Mrs. Roff) in tears that Lurancy Vennum was soon coming back and take possession of the body again. During all this time whenever Mary was asked where Lurancy was she would reply: 'Gone out somewhere' or 'in heaven', etc.

Mary, having informed her family that at eleven o'clock on May 21st, she would evacuate the body, which was now cured of its physical ailment, and Lurancy would come back into it, Mr. Roff wrote and mailed the following letter at ten o'clock—one hour before the predicted change in personality:

"Mary is to leave the body of Rancy (Lurancy) today about eleven o'clock, so she says. She is bidding neighbors and friends good-by. Rancy to return home all right today. Mary came from her room upstairs where she was sleeping with Lottie, last night and lay down beside us, hugged and kissed us, and cried because she must bid us good-by, telling us to give all her pictures, marbles and cards, and twenty-five cents Mrs. Vennum had given her, to Rancy, and had us promise to visit Rancy often. She tells me to write to Dr. Stevens as follows: Tell him I am going to heaven, and Rancy is coming home well . . . She said weeping, 'Oh pa I am going to heaven tomorrow at eleven o'clock and Rancy is coming back cured and going home (to Vennums) all right. She talked most lovingly about the separation to take place and most beautiful was her talk about heaven and home . . ."

As eleven o'clock came Mary seemed loath to give up the body and let Lurancy come back, but the transference took place at the stated time and the old consciousness of Lurancy again controlled it. At eleven-thirty Mr. Roff again wrote:

150

" . . . I mailed you a letter at half-past ten o'clock . . . She (Lurancy) wanted me to take her home, which I did. She called me Mr. Roff and talked with me as a young girl would not being acquainted. I asked her how things appeared to her—if they seemed natural. She said it seemed like a dream to her. She met her parents and brother in a very affectionate manner, hugging and kissing each one in tears of gladness. I saw her father just now and he says she has been perfectly natural and seems entirely well. You see my faith in writing you yesterday morning instead of waiting till she came."

The reader must by all means bear in mind that what I have related here is but a brief, very incomplete sketch of what took place, and that in its entirety the story is of great detail and significance. It was fully vouched for as well as the reputation of the persons involved, especially Mr. Roff who was the main narrator and witness and Dr. Stevens. The newspapers of the vicinity all gave attention to the occurrence and reported the news on it fully at the time, and as the events transpired; while several Court Judges, attorneys, business men and the mayor of the village furnished their testimonials.

This case has always been a "thorn in the side" of orthodox psychologists. Their theory of a "dual personality"—of a *split* in the mind appears inane. If nothing is in the mind except those things entering it through the medium of the five senses, where did Mary Roff's consciousness build from? Some psychologists try to invent miracles to explain away plain facts. Had the intelligent control Mary Roff have said: "I am merely a character created by a spirit in Lurancy's sub-conscious mentality," the psychologists would quote it far and wide. But that is not what she claimed. Mary Roff claimed to be the spirit of Mary Roff and nothing more.

I would submit this question: If, as some of our psychologists claim, in dual personality cases, the mind can create a perfect secondary personality, why does it not create a secondary personality which is duplicate of some living mortal's consciousness? Why is it a duplicate of a former (dead) person's consciousness?

Just as Dr. William McDougall was forced to the tentive conclusion that "Sally" in the Beauchamp case was a spirit* so was Dr. Hodgson similarly convinced that the case of Lurancy Vennum belonged to the spiritistic category.

Imagine a girl, dead twelve years, coming back, proving her identity, and living in the body of someone else! To the spiritualists this case stands as a classic example which portrays their teachings of healing, clairvoyance, survival, obsession, etc.

But the point which most concerns us here is this: Where was the spirit of Lurancy Vennum? Evidently there is but one answer—it was exteriorized, projected from her physical body, and existing in another world. It was just where the admitted intelligence known as Mary Roff said:—"Gone out somewhere."

AN ANSWER TO RICHET'S OBJECTIONS

The only serious attempt to dispose of the phenomenon of astral projection to come forth within the past forty years, aside from Mr. Podmore's 'telepathic hallucination' theory was published in a book *Our Sixth Sense*, in 1929 (Rider) by the late Charles Richet, in which that eminent Professor believed he was setting forth a great discovery. As he himself said: "This is a new chapter in psychology I claim to be writing."

Richet would have the world believe that he had discredited entirely the theory of astral projection in relation to so-called "hallucinations," (ghosts of the living) etc. His theory was simply this:

"The real world sends out vibrations around us. Some of them are perceived by our senses: others, not perceptible to our senses, are disclosed by our scientific instruments: but there are still

---

*See, *The Dissociation of a Personality*, by Morton Prince, and the S. P. R. Proceedings, Vol. XIX, pp 410-431.

others, perceived neither by our senses nor by our scientific in-
struments which act upon certain minds and reveal to them
fragments of reality."

Now as a matter of fact there is nothing extraordinary in such
a deduction and his theory is the result of very elementary
reasoning. He could easily have deducted thus: (1) I cannot
deny these occurrences take place. (2) Telepathy alone will
not cover the facts. (3) I ignore the astral body theory. Therefore I must *presume* the object, event, or person perceived sends
out an energy—a vibration; and, since the (seeing of) knowledge could not reach the percepient through the medium of the
five senses, I must add another. Consequently my result is (1) a
vibration of reality and (2) a sixth sense—neither of which can
be explained.

As I stated, this is obvious but a deduction, very elementary
reasoning and purely suppositional, especially the "vibration"
part of it. Aside from imparting a savor of great egotism in his
work, at every opportunity the Professor denounces the astral
body theory, but each time he does so, promptly retreats to safe
ground by making such remarks as "I do not care to discuss it."
The keynote to Richet's work is quickly discovered: -to idolize
his newly thought-up idea and ignore all else.

He states (p. 22) that survival is a *theory*—that the existence
of spirits is pre-supposed—and for that reason he will not discuss it because he deals in facts only, that the astral body (p. 49)
is an audacious hypothesis; that the astral body (p. 52) theory
is idle and futile to discuss. Again, that there is no motive
for invoking the spiritistic hypothesis; that this hypothesis
apparently contradicts the most precise and definite data
of psychology.

Yet the same Richet—who says the spirit hypothesis is unworthy of discussion and pre-supposed—that he deals in facts
alone—turns deliberately around and admits his so-called vibration of reality must be pre-supposed and is absolutely unknown and inexplicable!

He deals only in facts, according to p. 22, p. 48, and elsewhere, but on p. 10 says: "I frankly acknowledge the existence of a sixth sense is something very vague and cloudy." It must be something like a ghost. But Richet resents "ghosts" so we will conceive of his "vibration of reality" as a presumption, and his sixth sense as a vague and cloudy fact.

Commenting on the Verity case (p.101) he says: "There is nothing to prove that S. H. B.'s ghost, or astral body, manifested itself objectively." This is quite true and equally as true that there is nothing to prove Richet's theory covers the case.

Concerning the same case Richet calls the *will* of S. H. B. the *vibration of reality.* His contention is that it is all the same force or vibration of reality whether dealing with *inanimate objects* or *thought.* That is, if a percepient sees a house or other inanimate object, it is the vibration from the object which he sees. And if S. H. B. *wills* himself to appear to Miss Verity, the *will* of S. H. B.—his thought—is the vibration.

Now note this: In the Verity case Richet says *thought is the vibration* (p. 101) and yet on p. 208 he says he "would sooner believe it was the writing, the name, the event, which vibrates and *not thought.*" In attempting to explain the Verity case he has consigned his "new chapter in psychology" way back to the days of Mr. Podmore's thought transference. Such contradiction proves beyond a doubt that his whole theory is a pure speculation.

While the master mind F. W. H. Myers wrote pages and pages on probable explanations for collective hallucinations, Richet disposes of the Verity case, in its collective aspects in fourteen words, qualified by *may:*—"the sixth sense *may* function by calling up the same image in two minds."

In trying to explain what he admits is a "hypothesis of a vibration of reality" (p. 208)—and admits it in capital letters— he says:"This is an *attempt* (a provisional one, of course) at a *theory* of metapsychical knowledge." Mind you, this is an *attempt at a theory.* And in spite of the fact that he states time after time that he does not discuss theory, that he deals only in facts! Spiritism is unworthy of discussion because it is an audacious *theory!* It seems the vogue to overlook inconsistency if it comes from a scientist with a long list of degrees affixed to his signature.*

However, Richet is not always inconsistent, he does express *fact* when he says on p. 212 of his sixth sense, that it is a "new psychological notion."

Again he reaffirms: "I remain matter of fact and make no hypothesis" and constantly insists that he deals in facts alone; that, therefore the spiritistic idea is out of the question, but now once more he contradicts himself (p. 224) with the assertion: "We have dared to say that it was a matter of vibration. Of course that is a *hypothesis* . . . Let us then *assume* the hypothesis of vibration, and not admit the other hypothesis" (the spiritistic).

In the fore part of his work Richet says in effect that the astral body theory appears more simple—but that is no reason for accepting it.

Near the close of his work he contends his theory is more simple—that it should therefore be accepted.

The Professor tells us that we should place little credence in *observation* or statements related by others who witnessed certain psychic phenomena, because observations become distorted —added to and subtracted from—in the individual's mind. Still a goodly share of his book is devoted to building up his case on the observations of himself and others—even on dreams and hallucinations!

He maintains that his "new psychological notion" would eliminate the necessity of infering an astral body and for that reason it is futile to discuss the latter.

---

*Some scientists, like Richet, have the opinion that if they can concoct a theory which *could* account for a phenomenon, that it therefore *does* account for it.

He also maintains that his "notion" eliminates the inference of telepathy—but he *does* discuss the latter. Richet here surely proves he carries a "grudge" against the astral body theory.

On page 225 he tells us further that in dealing with ectoplasms, materializations, levitations, ghosts walking around, etc., the phenomena "depend upon a small number of subjects whose honesty is problematical." This can be nothing short of an insult to many spiritualists. I only hope their honesty never becomes as problematical as Richet's logic.

Richet asks (p. 52): "Is the hypothesis of a ghost, or astral body becoming materialized and traversing space more probable than that of a special indeterminate vibration?"

First he belittles our (believers in spirit) intelligence, then insults us, then asks our opinion on a question which is a deliberate misstatement of facts. The misstatement being *"an astral body becoming materialized and traversing space."* I challenge all followers of Richet to cite one single instance where such a contention is made by spiritists.

Of course, this sort of twisting of phraseology, coupled with such catchy adjectives as "a phantom in flesh and bone" (p. 52) help Richet along in his desire to humiliate the astral body hypothesis, but scientific honesty is not a matter of advancing one theory by misrepresenting its opposing theory. A medium resorting to such tactics would be promptly charged with fraud or perhaps his honesty would be considered problematical.

In condemning Dessoir for ridiculing the experiments of Mrs. Piper, Richet says (p. 196): "He (Dessoir) attempts to be impartial, and yet he follows the detestable method of many of our opponents, i. e. instead of grappling with the most favorable experiments he deals with the least favorable."

And that is exactly what Richet does when trying to evade the spiritistic hypothesis—picks out and discusses only incidents most favorable to his theory and refuses to go into the more significant problems. Is this a case of the pot calling the kettle *black?*

156

Although Richet contends that psychical manifestations are distorted by the mind of the witness, he, telling of an experiment he witnessed over fifty years before—which he offers as evidence supporting his theory—says: "I remember it as though it happened yesterday!"

When he comes to a discussion of *premonitions* (p. 184) which he admits occur, it is easily seen that Richet senses the futility of his explanation. Though he stoutly insists on p. 52 that "all groups of facts must admit of the same explanation" (which is anything but true)* the ardor of his explanation seems to die out when it clashes with premonitions.

He devotes two small paragraphs to the subject in which he states that, "in all *probability* premonition is also connected with the sixth sense" and that "to remain faithful to the programme we will say nothing about premonitions."

The reader will note that Richet does not even mention his so-called "vibration of reality" in this connection. Here is the reason why:—In premonition—where things seen occur in the future—there can be *no* vibration of reality; because the thing seen is not yet in reality and consequently can send out no vibration of reality. Denying higher planes of mind, Richet's theory now strikes a stone wall. Little wonder he prefers not to discuss the matter.

Sifted down, Richet's wonderful discovery, his new chapter in psychology, is a *supposition* of a 'vibration of reality' on the one hand and a mild admission of superconscious resources of mind on the other hand; the latter being a long established belief among thousands of enlightened people, and nothing new.

In truth, Richet himself is forced to admit in the conclusion

---

*Here is where I disagree with most of the researchers in this line. I say that a single fact sometimes admits of several explanations, e. g. *ghosts of the living* may be accounted for on several different theories and not one alone. S. M.

of his book that "there is perhaps a seventh, an eighth sense.'
Is that not synonymous with "superconsciousness"? How can
consciousness be separated from the senses or the senses function without mind? Scientific pride, of course, restrains Richet
from using the words "superconscious mind," so he ventures
forth with sixth, seventh, and eighth senses,—it sounds more
scientific.

We must not criticise Richet too strongly for these contra-
dictions and evasions, for he was a human being, and like all of
us, guided to a great extent by his emotions—his desires and
sentiments. Often we believe ourselves to be using logic when
we are really only expressing our inner sentiments, sometimes
quite unconsciously. We can always depend upon our minds to
evolve a chain of argument to defend those things we enjoy, or
ridicule those things we oppose. And we often do this without
understanding the true underlying reason. So it was, I believe,
with Richet; I feel his arguments against the spiritistic hypothesis show at every hand that they were expressions, not of actual
logic, but of sentiment.

I ask my readers now to overlook the contradictory statements of Professor Richet, which it has been necessary for me to
point out in setting forth my case for astral projection, and let
us pay tribute to his memory as a fearless, out-spoken human
being who had the courage at least to investigate and admit
certain psychical phenomena really did occur—even though
we may not agree with his explanations at all times. Let us be
glad that he lived.

WAS MRS. PIPER PROJECTED?

Probably the most remarkable, most scientifically investigated, and best attested case of trance mediumship in the history
of psychical science is that of Mrs. Piper. Her case was so
thoroughly gone into and extensively chronicled by such eminent persons as Dr. Hodgson, F. W. H. Myers, Professor James,

Professor Newbold, Professor Hyslop, Dr. Walter Leaf, Sir Oliver Lodge, and so many many other trustworthy and honest investigators who have written voluminously their reports on it, that I am sure the great majority of my readers already know the full history of it.

Newcomers into the psychic field would profit greatly by a thorough study of the original reports; but to give those particular persons a vague idea of what took place during Mrs. Piper's trances, I quote in abbreviated form from Dr. Hodgson's report in Vol. XXXIII of the S. P. R. *Proceedings*:

" . . . She seems to be partly conscious, as it were, of two worlds . . . She sees figures and hears voices before she has completely lost her consciousness." When in deep trance she seems to "possess, not the dreamy consciousness of the previous stage—partly aware of two worlds—but a fuller and clearer consciousness . . . which is in direct relation, however, not so much with our ordinary physical world, as with another world . . . What I believe happens is that *Mrs. Piper's normal or supraliminal consciousness becomes in some way dormant, and that her subliminal consciousness withdraws completely from the control of her body and takes her supraliminal consciousness with it.*

". . . The upper part of her body tends to fall forward, and I support her head with cushions on a table. About this time, or shortly afterwards . . . the right arm manifests a *control* by what seems to be another consciousness and begin to make movements suggesting writing . . . The upper part of the body, including the left arm is then usually controlled by one personality and the right arm by another . . . The personalities controlling respectively the hand and the voice showed apparently a complete independence. (Dr. Phinuit controlled the voice; George Pelham, the hand) . . . Whether 'spirits' as they assert, or not, Phinuit and the other consciousness controlling the hand appear to be entirely distinct from each other, and frequently carry on separate conversations—simultaneous and independent—with different sitters. . . . The writing produced is very different from Mrs. Piper's ordinary writing.

" . . . The hand behaves at times as though one consciousness withdrew from the hand to make room for another; and at other times as though the sudden arrival of another 'indirect communicator' nearly ousted the direct communicator from the hand . . ."

As to the question of fraud, Professor James, in *The Psychological Review*, states that he implicitly agreed with all other investigators of Mrs. Piper, that such a hypothesis was entirely out of the question, and goes on to say:

"The medium has been under observation, much of the time under close observation, as to most of the conditions of her life, by a large number of persons, eager, many of them, to pounce upon any suspicious circumstance for fifteen years. During that time, not only has there been not one single suspicious circumstance remarked, but not one suggestion has ever been made from any quarter which might tend positively to explain how the medium, living the life she leads, could possibly collect information about so many sitters by natural means."

Professor James continues: "The scientist who is confident of fraud here, must remember that in science as much as in common life a hypothesis must receive some positive specification and determination before it can be profitably discussed, and a fraud which is no assigned kind of fraud, but simply 'fraud' at large, fraud *in abstracto,* can hardly be regarded as a specially scientific explanation of concrete facts . . . "

There were three periods of time and three differing conditions manifested during Mrs. Piper's trances:

(1)   From the years 1884 to 1891 the dominant controlling personality (claiming to be a disembodied spirit) known as *Dr. Phinuit* who used the vocal organs almost exclusively.

(2)   From 1892 to 1896 when another control (claiming also to be a spirit) known as George Pelham communicated

160

chiefly by automatic writing—although the major control (Dr. Phinuit) also communicated by speech during the same period.

(3) Where other alleged spirits of the dead supervised and communicated mostly by automatic writing, but occasionally by speech.

During these trances an abundance of supernormal information was given out to the sitters present, by these alleged spirit controls of Mrs. Piper—information which could be checked and proved. While I would enjoy relating some of these communications, space forbids, so in this connection I refer especially to Vol. XIII of the S. P. R. *Proceedings.*

Now aside from the conclusions of many of the investigators, such as the statement of Dr. Hodgson that he believed that Mrs. Piper's entire mentality—conscious and unconscious—withdrew from her body, there are many other incidents which would bring us to the conclusion that her spiritual body actually exteriorized or projected from its physical counterpart during these trances.

Is it not a curious coincidence that noises such as *snapping, cracking, clicking,* etc., especially in the head, should be heard by persons at the moment they claim to have exteriorized or interiorized when having an out-of-the-body experience—while noises of the same character are described as occurring when Mrs. Piper had her trances?

In this book you will find reference to many such noises in the various accounts. For instance, Mrs. Brewster says: "There was a *zinging* in my ears and in a moment I sat up breathless in my physical body." Mr. Edgerton says: "To my ears came a note, corresponding to the middle E on a piano." In the account captioned *Walks on air, Sees Physical Body,* the narrator says: "There came a flashing of lights in my eyes and a *ringing* in my ears." Mr. Gerhardi says: "It seemed to me as if a

161

dozen coolies, among much *screeching* and *throbbing were* lowering some precious burden which was myself." Oliver Fox tells of a *cerebral click* as he found himself back in his body. Mr. Pelley says: "A long, swift swirling journey . . . and then something *clicked*. Something in my body. The best analogy is the sound my repeating deer-rifle makes when I work the ejector mechanism—a flat metallic sensation . . . " Dr. Wilste stated that he "felt and heard the snapping of innumerable small cords."

I discussed these noises in *The Projection of the Astral Body* and said, in part: " . . . A peculiar noise which seems close to the ear or inside the head. A very common one is 'pop!' as if a toy balloon burst close to the ear. Another is a loud 'sizz,' and sometimes a sound inside the brain, causing that organ to vibrate. Another is a *cracking* sound, not unlike the noise made by an electric spark when the positive and negative posts of a battery are touched together. This sound is usually heard just at the take-off of projection as well as at the moment of re-coincidence, and seems to be in the head, near the back part of the skull.

"Still another kind of sound commonly heard is a *zing* as if a string were tightly drawn through the head and then struck, as one might strike the strings of a guitar . . . The striking thing about these noises is the way in which they can be *felt*—yes, actually felt—moving inside of one's skull; one's brain seems to shake like the diaphragm of a drum which vibrates when struck and resounds . . . "

Besides these head-noises testified to by those claiming to have been out of their bodies, the reader will recall the very large number of instances in which the projected phantom saw the astral cord. IS IT BUT ANOTHER COINCIDENCE THAT MRS. PIPER WOULD MENTION NOT ONLY THE *SNAPP-ING NOISES* BUT ALSO THE *CORD?*

On one occasion when coming out of trance she said: "They (meaning the spirit controls) are going away, too bad—'snap.'"

162

Of this, Sir Oliver Lodge remarked: "She refers to a sensation which she calls a *snap in the head,* which nearly always heralds a return to consciousness. Sometimes (the snapping sounds) herald almost a sudden return, and she is always more conscious after the *snap* than before; but often it takes two *snaps* to bring her to. What this *snap* is? I do not know but suspect it to be something physiological."

Professor Hyslop in his *Observations of Certain Trance Phenomena* (S. P. R. *Proceedings* VOL. XVI) states that "Mrs. Piper heard her head snap," and that she said to the sitters: "You heard my head *snap* didn't you? When my *head snaps* I can't tell you anything . . . "

NOW NOTICE THIS PASSAGE ESPECIALLY IN WHICH MRS. PIPER SPEAKS OF THREE OCCURRENCES COINCIDING WITH PROJECTION PHENOMENA, (1) *coming into her body*— (2) *head noises*— (3) *seeing the astral cord*:

"They (the spirits) were talking to me. I came in on a cord— a silver cord—another snap."

Again Mrs. Piper said: "A line—a line goes out from me to them." There are many such instances as these which strongly indicate a close relation between her trances and projection.

The *controls* too (who claimed to occupy her vacated physical shell) stated that they could *see the medium leaving and returning to her physical* body. For instance, Dr. Phinuit said to Sir Oliver Lodge (S. P. R. *Proceedings* Vol. VI, p516): "Captain, do you know when I came in, *I met the medium going out . . .* "

Lodge says that Phinuit, the major control "seems to give up his place for the other personality—friend or relative—who then communicates with something of his old manner and individuality." And in another instance Sir Oliver says: "It is quite as if he, in his turn, evacuated the body, just as Mrs. Piper had done, while a third personality uses it for a time."

Again Lodge continues: "While the dominating controls

163

know Mrs. Piper well—sometimes speak of seeing her going out as they are coming in—a *new* control does not know who she is or what she has to do with the business . . . sometimes the control speaks of having tried to grasp the 'spirit of light' (Mrs. Piper's luminous body) and give it a message as it was returning to the physical body."

In the S. P. R. Vol. XIII, pp308f, Dr. Hodgson states that George Pelham informed the sitter that he could not make Dr. Phinuit understand what he wanted him to say so he told the medium *just as she was returning to her body again.* On being informed that Mrs. Piper had delivered the message right after re-entering her physical body, Pelham remarked: "Good—you see, *I saw her spirit just as she was coming in* and as I could not tell Dr. Phinuit (the voice control) I took a chance."

In Vol. VIII of the *Proceedings* p. 130, *Dr. Phinuit* speaking to the sitter, Mr. Rich said: "Here is Newell, and he wants to talk to you 'Reach'—so I'll go about my business whilst you are talking and will come back later." Confusion followed and Mr. Rich claims he heard *Dr. Phinuit* say "Here, Newell, you come by the hands, while I go out by the feet."

When Professor James told Dr. Phinuit to force the medium's eye-balls into their normal waking position, he did so and then asserted that he had "got twisted round somehow and couldn't find his way out again."

Are those statements and testimonials not striking evidence in favor of the theory that man has a spirit and that under certain conditions it can be projected from the body? While I did not intend to set forth any of my own conclusions or opinions in this book, I am going to break that promise just once and say that I contend that this is a case in which the projection of the astral body figured.

For the life of me, I cannot understand how any intelligent person, admitting the Piper phenomena occurred at all, has the utter stupidity to grope around trying to find some flimsy theory to offer as a substitute for the spiritistic. Some of our so-called scientists must be indeed intoxicated by egotism, fear of ridicule, pride, or downright dogmatic antagonism, to admit this phenomena occurred, yet try to explain it away by a more unbelievable hypothesis than the spiritistic.

Even the arch-sceptic, Richet, who ired so many spiritualists, and never missed a chance to deny and disfavor the spiritistic hypothesis, was unwilling to make himself ridiculous by offering his "Sixth Sense" to fully cover the facts in the Piper case. Rather than admit this spiritistic hypothesis, he prefers not to discuss it much and only did to the extent of picking out a few instances which his theory might cover—and evade all the rest in a suave manner, and by fully defending himself in advance. In his last work of note (*Our Sixth Sense*) he says:

" . . . The facts relating to Mrs. Piper are probably the most important that have ever been obtained. At the risk of appearing too timid, we will not discuss the spiritistic hypothesis, although the experiments with Mrs. Piper frequently, though not always, admit more readily of a spiritistic explanation than of any other . . . "

When Mrs. Piper goes into trance, George Pelham says that "she passes out as your ethereal goes out when you sleep" . . . and after death "everything is expressed in thought . . . but necessarily, as you see, depend upon the body of another person or Ego in the material world to express one's thought fully, after the annihiliation of one's own material body . . . "

Suppose, for the sake of argument, that this control's true nature is a matter of speculation. If this intelligence was as a conscious individual, like a normal personality—reasonably sane and logical, precise, giving out truthful information,—then why, in the name of common sense would this intelligence claim to be a spirit, if it were not? If it were some other strata of mind, and was able to reason, why would it not say it was some other strata of mind? Why does he claim to be a spirit of the dead? He would have no reason for doing so!

165

I maintain that when the controls told the truth about other matters they told the truth about themselves—that they were dis-embodied spirits—and that they told the truth about Mrs. Piper—that she evacuated her body and they occupied it. I maintain that when Mrs. Piper claims to "see a cord—come into her body on a cord—hear her *head snap* and become conscious physically; that when Phinuit says "when I came in, I met the Medium going out," etc., etc.—the case is evidental testimony in favor of the projection of the astral body, and that therefore some of our greatest scientists have already corroborated this testimony, by their own admissions.

CONCLUSION

I now wish to make my position perfectly clear. While projection of the astral body must remain but a theory to those who have not experienced it, I am personally convinced beyond a doubt of its reality and of a posthumous existence.

Yet I do not maintain, as do many Spiritualists, that all psychical phenomena is to be attributed solely to spirit. Neither do I swing to the other extreme, as do many psychical researchers, and credit none to spirit. What I do maintain is that we have multiplex psychical phenomena and it admits of multiplex explanations—some spiritistic, some mental, some interdependent of both.

This is where I quarrel with most of my contemporaties, both Spiritualists and psychical researchers. As I stated at the beginning of this book that no single explanation will suffice to cover all cases, I again repeat that often one single psychical occurrence admits of several hypothesis; often several psychical occurrences seem covered by a single hypothesis; and often no hypothesis appears sufficient to cover a given occurrence.

The reader will readily see that while the supposition or hypothesis of telepathy or "vibration of reality" or the like, could easily be invoked, in absence of proof, as covering many instances where phantasms of the living have been seen, *that no other explanation but projection of the astral body will suffice to cover cases like those listed in part two of this book*

Again, there are cases which not one of the foregoing explanations will cover satisfactorily; cases, for instance, with a premonitional aspect, in which the percepient sees his own double. I cite a few:

167

Abraham Lincoln, for instance, shortly after his election in 1860 told of seeing two veritble ghosts of himself, simultaneously—but the face of one of them was "five shades paler" than that of the other.

The uncanny occurrence was interpreted by Mrs. Lincoln as a *sign* that he would be elected twice but would not live through his second term!

Percy Bysshe Shelley, on June 23, 1822 while living at Pisa, Italy saw his own phantom double. It bekoned to him and, although terrified, Shelley followed it down to the sea where he lost sight of it. Two weeks later Shelley was drowned in that very sea!

Then there was the case of Professor M. W. L. De Witte, the critic. The Professor says that he "saw his own ghost" walking in front of himself and entering the house where he lived. This caused him to turn back and go to a hotel for the night. Next morning when he returned home he found that the ceiling of his bedroom had fallen and buried the bed—where he would have slept—in a heap of rubbish!

Goethe, the mighty German, recounts an account of this nature which happened to himself, in two of his works, *Wahrheit und Dichtung* and *Aus Meinem Leben*. When he was twenty-one he said "goodby" to Fredericka Biron, the girl he loved, and rode sadly away from Sesenheim, in Alsace, the town where she lived. On reaching the path leading to Drusenheim he suddenly saw a phantom double of himself in a gray suit embroidered with gold, such as he had never worn before. The double was riding toward him and back toward the home of Fredericka. He watched the phantom until it vanished and declared it had a calming influence upon him in those unhappy moments following the parting.

"How strange", Goethe relates, that eight years later I found myself riding along the same road to visit Fredericka again, wearing the gray suit with gold trimmings that I had seen on the phantom double—and I wore it not by design, but by chance!"

Maurice Mæterlinck the world famous author, who claims to have had many premonitions, believes that they never fortell a fortunate event, yet many cases seem to contradict this, and my observation is that some appear to have a definite purpose while others fortell only something casual and of little real significance.

I would feel chagrined to offer the astral body theory as a definite explanation to cases like the foregoing. Certainly they cannot be explained by telepathy. And there was no "vibration from the real world about us", as Richet would have it, because, e. g. in the case of Goethe, the phantasmal double appeared eight years before the event took place in reality. There was the superconscious aspect too—that of being enabled to see the gray suit and gold trimmings.

Occurrences like these require, among other things, a study of the true nature of time and space (of the fourth dimension) which is outside the bounds of this work. So, in this connection I would refer to the valuable contribution to the subject *An Experiment With Time* by J. W. Dunne.*

But I caution my readers in advance, not to be led away by the assertions of Mr. Dunne against the astral body theory, merely because he is a scientist of high standing; for his assertions are, like Richet's, pre-supposed and obvious an expression of sentiment, not logic.

We are told that being a scientist, he could not entertain the idea of spirit, telepathy, clairvoyance, etc. In other words he had his mind made up, against the spiritistic hypothesis, in

---

*Mr. Dunne had numerous dreams in which he saw events which later occurred in the physical world. From those dreams, he evolved his hypothesis of *time* and *space*.

169

advance, and a biased mind cannot be truly impartially scientific. He says:

"There can be no reasonable doubt that the idea of a soul must have first arisen in the mind of primitive man as the result of observation of his dreams. Ignorant as he was he could have come to no other conclusion but that, in dreams, he felt his sleeping body in one universe and went wandering off in another. It is considered that, but for that savage, the idea of such a thing as a soul would never have even occurred to mankind; so that arguments subsequently introduced to bolster up a case thus *tainted at its source* can have no claim to anyone's serious attention."

Now any school-child knows that this is a personal supposition. How can Dunne or anyone else possibly know at this late date where the belief in a soul had its inception? He knows no more about where the belief originated than the ignorant savage of which he speaks. And it seems rather a startling paradox that while the belief in a soul is, according to Dunne, tainted at its source, mostly because it had its inception in dreams, that Mr. Dunne's wonderful discovery, claimed to be of "so significant a character as to effect our entire conception of human life" likewise had its inception in dreams—his dreams! *

I recall that Richet maintained the idea of immortality originated from a desire to continue living. The two great scientists disagree on a question which no one could possible know anything about! The truth is both were "guessing" and are pawning off their personal ideas in the name of science. Are we to presume from Dunne's own assertion that his theory of *time* and *space*—having had its inception in dreams—is tainted at its source and can have no claim to anyone's serious attention? And can he prove that he ever had a dream? No, he

---

*Notice that we are not founding our case for projection (part two) on dreams, but on consciousness.

170

cannot. Neither can persons claiming to have projected prove their statements; because both dreams and projections are subjective phenomena and only self-evident to the individual experiencing them.

So, while I heartily recommend Dunne's book as a study of 'out of time' psychical experiences there must be a separation of the wheat (facts) from the chaff (presumptions) and his work while laudable as a whole, like Richet's, does not disprove the astral body theory one iota.

It seems rather an amusing fact that while the idea of a spirit has persisted for centuries and centuries, the only argument which can be brought against it—even by first-rate scientists— is an expression of their own personal opinions and sentiments.

Viewed from the opposite angle, the fact must not be overlooked that such men as Crookes, Lodge, Wallace, and numerous other first-rank scientists famous the world over, have not hesitated to publicly announce their acceptance of the spiritistic hypothesis.

Undoubtedly the most extensive investigator of his time whose writings fairly bubble-over with profound logic and intricate analysis, was F. W. H. Myers, his unbiased attitude having been praised even by his strongest opponents. Myers says:

"These *self-projections* represent the most extraordinary achievements of the human will, and are perhaps acts which a man might perform equally well before and after death."

Although I could have greatly enlarged upon the evidence for astral projection, I feel that enough has now been set forth to convince the average reader that we are dealing with a phenomenon which is anything but mythical.

The testimony of ten persons claiming to have experienced a certain occurrence should carry far more weight than the denial of ten thousand persons admitting they know nothing about the subject. So to this latter class—those who deny—I ask: How can you deny that which you admit you know nothing of? Because you have not experienced projection of the astral body does not prove that no one else has.

In a court of law your opinions on a case would be thrown out as worthless if you knew nothing of the case. You could not even get upon the witness chair; and only those persons claiming to have knowledge of the case would be qualified as witnesses.

I have presented my witnesses and *their experiences cannot be explained except by the projection of the astral body.* If you cannot accept their word, whom would you expect to accept yours, were you to undergo a definitely describable conscious experience?

Sir Oliver Lodge has pointed out that *denial* is no more infallible than *assertion.* Our courts of justice are functioning upon this principle. And, after all, is it not a remarkable coincidence that so many people claim to have *seen* phantoms of the living, while so many others claim to have *been* phantoms of the living?

By presenting the testimony of the latter group, I maintain that we have an air-tight case for the projection of the astral body, which cannot be credited to any other explanation. This reminds me of what the noted English writer H. Ernest Hunt— who collected a number of cases similar to those I have set down in part two—said:

"The tales they tell are essentially the same, and unless one is quite gratiously to assume that they are all telling lies, and more wonderful still, the same lie, it is only reasonable to suppose they tell the truth."

And, once we admit the reality of the projection of the astral body we are forced to a conclusion similar to that of G. R. S. Mead, who long ago wrote:

"In my opinion, it is this . . . subtle body idea, which for so many centuries has played the dominant role in the traditional psychology of both the East and the West, that is most deserving of being retried, reviewed, and revised, to serve as a working hypothesis to co-ordinate and explain a very large number of these puzzling psychical phenomena."

CPSIA information can be obtained at www.ICGtesting.com
Printed in the USA
LVOW082028210113

316601LV00002B/479/A